How to put a new kind of fun and joy into your life

1) Turn on the music, and you're ready to go.

2) Swing into the rhythms of *Jazzercise*.

3) Loosen up your tension, tighten and tone your muscles. Exercising to the beat of jazz helps you dance your troubles away—and the inches, too.

JAZZERCISE®

JAZZERCISE®

Rhythmic Jazz Dance-Exercise

A Fun Way To Fitness

by Judi Missett
with Dona Z. Meilach

Photography by
Dona and Mel Meilach

RL 9, IL 9+

JAZZERCISE®

A Bantam Book / April 1978
2nd printing . . . . . June 1980

ISBN 0-553-14397-2

Published simultaneously in the United States and Canada

Bantam Books are published by Bantam Books, Inc. Its trade-
mark, consisting of the words ''Bantam Books'' and the por-
trayal of a bantam, is Registered in U.S. Patent and Trademark
Office and in other countries. Marça Registrada. Bantam
Books, Inc., 666 Fifth Avenue, New York, New York 10019.

PRINTED IN THE UNITED STATES OF AMERICA

11 10 9 8 7 6 5 4 3 2

FOR JACK AND SHANNA

"Energy is a source of sheer delight."
Friedrich Wilhelm Nietzsche
(1844–1900)

Acknowledgments

We wish to thank the following people who have helped in the preparation of this book:

- The students in all of Judi's classes who offered the opportunity, encouragement, and appreciation of the techniques she developed.
- The dancers in Chapter 9 who enthusiastically performed in their various costumes.
- Margarite Neumann of Margarite Neumann Studio of Classical Ballet, Vista, California, for the use of her studio for the photography sessions.
- Anna Wolf for her special help, her many creative suggestions, and her invaluable editing assistance.
- Our husbands, Jack Missett and Mel Meilach, for assistance, encouragement, and for being there whenever we needed them, beyond the call of any marriage contract.
- Judi's dad and mom—Del and June Sheppard—for all the dancing lessons.
- Connie Williams for her neat, expressive drawings.
- Dr. Mel Pollack for putting us in touch with each other in the first place.
- Marilyn Regula and Anna Wolf for typing the final manuscript.

Judi Sheppard Missett, Vista, California
Dona Meilach, San Diego, California

Contents

Introduction

It's exciting to be part of a trend toward physical fitness and an integrating of mind, spirit, and body. Many excellent dancers, physical educators, specialists in body language, and sports persons are working to expand awareness of the body, its inner messages, and how it communicates the experience of life.

This book concentrates on a special technique of movement and dance which helps many people to reacquaint themselves with their bodies and the energy that is always within. The dancing and dance exercises described are basic movements which can be expanded upon and used creatively by you at home, or by teachers, physical educators, and specialists. However you choose to use the material, I hope that the exhilarating feel of a fit body and the joy of dancing that I have always known will be yours.

Judi Sheppard Missett

Jazzercise

Judi does a jazz-rock stomp movement.

When was the last time you moved like a child? Running, jumping, hopping, skipping—and felt *so good* doing it! Have you been searching for a way to feel that good again—a way to exercise that isn't exercise? An escape route from kicking your legs in predictable movements to the count of 1, 2, 3, 4?

Grown-ups seem to leave behind the joyful movements that were part of everyday life as youngsters—and were good for them too! But there is a way to recapture this. It's so beautiful you'll wonder why you haven't discovered it earlier, and it's fun! It will reacquaint you with your body and make your body your friend.

It's Jazzercise! The latest body conditioning approach that is gaining followers as if the Pied Piper were playing the music. Jazzercise uses jazz dance steps, and when put together, they become jazz dance routines. They are all done with the best music on record—music that motivates your body to set itself into motion.

Jazz dance is partly a revival of the Fred Astaire and Ginger Rogers routines performed in the 1930s when the whole world was hopping and jumping on dance floors. But today's jazz dance is more than a nostalgic revival. It's an updated, delightful debut using dance steps and music to help your heart beat better and make your body more fit. By bouncing to a "boogie beat" in a planned way, you'll dance inches away and your body will be more flexible than you ever dreamed possible.

Need proof? Sign up for one of the growing numbers of jazz dance-exercise classes that are becoming popular at dance studios, YMCAs, in local recreation department programs, in college extension courses, and wherever people are concerned about body conditioning.

The first time you see a class of this kind in action, you might groan a little and tell yourself, "I could never do that!" Not true. That initial reaction is quickly dispelled by a first session. Each stretch, each movement is gradual. Your muscles will cooperate as they get the message that these movements are what they have been demanding for years. A little stiffness at first? Undoubtedly. But within a few days, they'll be aching to *move* when the mood of the music motions them to stretch and kick. You'll feel loose, limber, and want to let yourself go. You'll discover that your body *can* do those things you never thought it could. Have you seen the kicks dancers do in a chorus line? You'll be able to do them too, as gracefully and confidently as though you were on stage.

You practically are! For you can do your jazzercises and dance steps anywhere. Your living-room floor is your stage. Your audience is your mirror. Your radio, record player, or tape set is your band. You don't need any other equipment or machinery; you need only the mood and the motivation, often provided by a first look in the mirror at the inches that you want to lose.

You will become positively addicted to this new way of moving because it puts a joyful bounce in your step and a smile on your face! You will also be able to share your knowledge of the latest songs and dance steps with your friends—the very same songs and dance steps they have heard and seen on television, in nightclubs, and on the stage.

The dance steps, movements, and much of the music utilized in the jazzercise program have been adapted from the American jazz dance world. And, as you become involved in it, you will want to know more about the background and development of American jazz—how it all began and how it influences today's music and movement.

Jazz music and jazz dance parallel one another in a humble, gradual beginning, and they form an important part of American culture. Their heritage is traced to the rhythms and movements brought here by black slaves. This developed into the black music of the early 1900s: church hymns, brass bands, spirituals, and the blues. White performers often imitated the black movements and rhythms to create dances of their own. Little by little, these rhythms and movements appeared on stage as "buck and wing" and "clog" dances in minstrel and early vaudeville shows.

It all seemed to burst out in the twenties with the Charleston, the dance that put the whole nation hopping on its toes and wiggling its fingers. All kinds of dances followed in drum-beatlike succession: the Big Apple, the Black Bottom, and the Castle Walk—named for its creators, Vernon and Irene Castle.

By the 1930s, jazz was an important and pervading musical concept. Its interpretation in dance, characterized by

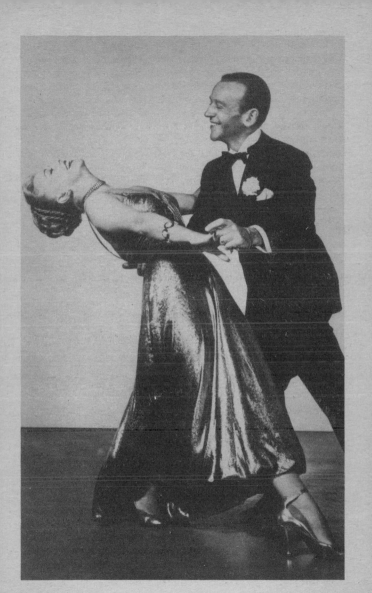

Ginger Rogers and Fred Astaire dazzled the country with their perfectly choreographed and performed dance routines.

fastpaced, high-stepping performances, spread around the world in movies made popular by extravaganza producer Busby Berkeley, and by dancers such as Ginger Rogers and Fred Astaire.

At the same time, the black American bands of Duke Ellington and Louis Armstrong began to attract the attention of dance musicians. It was "New Orleans coming up the Mississippi to Chicago" jazz, first popularized by the Original Dixieland Jazz Band, then recorded by Joseph "King" Oliver and by "Jelly Roll" Morton's Red Hot Peppers. And when Duke Ellington wrote "It Don't Mean a Thing if It Ain't Got That Swing," the Swing Era was born. It was the time of the big bands—Artie Shaw, Glen Miller, and Benny Goodman—vocalists like the Andrews Sisters, and dances like the Peabody, the Jitterbug, and the Boogie Woogie.

In the middle forties, jazz dance inevitably found its place on the Broadway stage. In *Fancy Free* and, later, *On the Town*, dance sequences choreographed by Jerome Robbins delighted audiences with a shift from classical and contemporary dance to a newer, freer, more rhythmic form of movement. In 1951, the film *An American in Paris* and, in 1954, the Broadway production of *Pajama Game* continued to use this new jazz style.

In the late forties, and on through the fifties, another name began to gain the respect of dance audiences—Jack Cole. From his performing company came the talented dancers Gwen Verdon and Carol Haney. Cole's style was unique, creative, imaginative, and highly exciting. He used material from the ballet, from Oriental, Hindu, Latin, and Harlem cultures to give a tense, high-paced electrifying flavor to his choreography. Mr. Cole could easily be called the innovator of modern jazz movement and technique—the father of jazz dance. He paved the way for choreographers like Bob Fosse (*Chicago*) and Michael Bennett (*A Chorus Line*).

Jack Cole once said that real jazz dance is "urban folk dance," but it must always have that essence of feeling for the music, of individual expression. Another jazz artist expressed it in another way. When asked, "What is jazz?" he answered succinctly, "Baby, if you gotta ask, you ain't got it!"

Jack Cole and Jerome Robbins were the first choreographers to build dances into the structure of jazz. George Balanchine brought jazz dance to the concert stage with his *Slaughter on Tenth Avenue*, followed by Composer Robert Prince and

4   JAZZERCISE

Gene Kelly introduced a variety of high-stepping, acrobatic dances filled with innovative choreography. Here he is with Sharon McManus in the movie *Anchors Aweigh*.

Jerome Robbins's *New York Export: Opus Jazz*, and a segment of Robbins's *Ballets: U.S.A.* In 1957, Jerome Robbins and Leonard Bernstein's *West Side Story* was heralded as a landmark in American musical theater. This was the musical that gave jazz dance to the American public.

Something else happened in the fifties to further change jazz music and dance. It was Rock and Roll, and it did just that— it rocked the whole scene! Dances like the Chicken, the Stroll, the Hucklebuck, and the Hully Gully encouraged the whole country to get back up on the dance floor, and it did.

Bob Dylan sang "The Times They Are A-Changin'," and it was the 1960s. With them came long hair, protests, marches, a "do-your-own-thing" attitude, and discotheques with dances like the Frug, the Twist, the Monkey, and the Pony. Television shows *Hullabaloo* and *Shindig* featured these and other emerging dances. And in the late 1960s, an even freer, more innovative dance style was seen in the popular musical *Hair*. By this time, the public had become aware of and comfortable with the many styles emerging and melting into jazz dance—that of the rock-and-roll dancer, the musical comedy dancer, the nightclub Las Vegas-style dancer, and the television dancer.

In the early 1970s, discotheque was replaced by "disco," which is characterized by an individual, artistic self-expression. This gave rise to dances like the Hustle, the Bus Stop, the Bump, the Roller Coaster, and the New Cha-Cha. Many of these are more choreographed and fancier than ever before, and there is a certain skill required to do them well. It is this skill, along with increasing interest in a new approach to physical fitness, which is responsible for the growing popularity of jazz dance-exercise.

Among the many exciting characteristics of jazz dance is that it is ever changing. It takes its personality from the tempo and music of the time. Gus Giordano, a nationally known dancer-teacher from the Midwest, summed it up when he said, "Modern jazz is as American as hot dogs. It has been accepted by the American public . . . sensing this jazz dance fever . . . an American expression which is winning friends and disciples for us all over the world."

The sequences in this book emphasize some of the technical aspects of jazz dance. They are designed to complement classes already being offered around the country by dancers well trained in jazz dance technique. Whether you learn the steps and movements on your own, or in a class, you'll find that you're shaping up and enjoying it all more.

The jazzercise habit happens once you discover the fun of fancy footwork and the joy of new-found energy. You will take the time to fit it into the busiest schedule. Who knows? You may even be inspired to get involved with a small performing group or perhaps organize a dance group of your own.

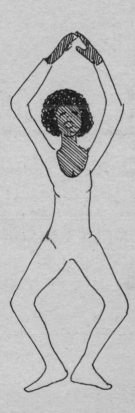

Jump into Jazz!

We've stressed the fun and some of the benefits involved when you jazzercise. You've learned a bit of jazz dance history. But there are other reasons to begin a jazz dance-exercise program. Men and women who have jumped on the jazz bandwagon tell it best:

A thirty-two-year-old jazzercise enthusiast says: "I look forward to the classes. The movements are novel, always different when set to a variety of musical selections. Dancing throws my troubles away. It does wonders for my mind and spirit."

A fortyish advertising executive comments: "A dance session after work releases the day's tensions and frustrations. I feel the furrows in my forehead disappearing. I find myself smiling, laughing every time I jump and kick. I leave the class with a new-found buoyancy."

"That buoyancy is energy," says the mother of three teenagers who keep her hopping. "Since I've been dancing, I can keep up with my kids. I also know the same music they know, the groups and songs. They tell me I'm 'with it' and I love it."

"There's even more to it than renewed energy," observes a young couple, both involved in jazzercise. "It spills over into everything we do. The way we walk, play tennis, swim, even our sex life. We can stretch, and enjoy the potentials of our bodies in every aspect."

And many women agree with what one lady put so aptly: "I've always fantasized myself as a chorus girl. This is my chance to live out my fantasies."

So you see, anybody can jazzercise, from youngsters who visualize themselves in the Olympics on the parallel bars to senior citizens who want to stay active and healthy. There is no age limit to motivation.

The beauty of jazz dancing is that underneath the fun and music, the point of it all is cardiovascular (heart and lungs), muscular, metabolic (body chemistry), and emotional improvement. A happy body is a healthy body! It's all planned into the movements and comes so subtly you may not realize what's happening. Here is how it works:

Your body is actually divided into sections. The jazzercises that follow are designed to tone each section, beginning with the head and moving down to the toes, until every area is explored. A specific routine might concentrate particularly on strengthening the cardiovascular system, but balance and coordination are also required to perform it. Another routine might focus on trimming the thighs, but the exercise also adds to leg flexibility . . . since the leg bone is connected to the knee bone, and so on.

Jazzercise conditions you totally; it improves balance, coordination, flexibility, muscle tone, stamina, posture, and, most importantly, it lifts your spirit by releasing unwanted tension and blocked energy. It reaffirms the positive, pleasant side of your personality.

Convinced? Then let's get down to the happy business at hand, for the word "dance" conjures up happy feelings. If you've got a little ham in you, all the better. Jazz dancing is joyful dancing; at the same time, it's fitness with a flair!

What to Wear

You can entertain that muse to dance with a flair in what you wear too. You'll move better, and with more confidence, when you wear clothes that look neat and professional. Outfits that let you move freely, such as T-shirts and shorts and exercise warm-up suits, are suitable for both men and women. For women, leotards and tights are suggested.

There are many attractive, practical leotard styles available. They come in short sleeves, cap sleeves, long sleeves, and sleeveless, camisoles, and turtlenecks. Those with zippered fronts and backs are practical for performing; however, they may be uncomfortable when doing floor movements. New fabrics, such as Milliskin, are nice for a slick, shiny, clingy look. All leotards can become the basis for dance costumes should your involvement lead you into actual performances with a dance group. (See Chapter 9 for more ideas about costumes and performances.)

Tights can match or contrast with your leotards. Stirrup-type tights wear longer than those with feet, and they permit more freedom since they don't slip on the floor. Those with feet should be worn with shoes to prevent slipping. Support tights made by Danskin are nice for performing and for general appearance; they hold the leg firmly and give a smooth, neat line. Mesh tights are not recommended as they may dig into your knees and legs.

For the standing exercises, shoes are optional. You can wear tennis shoes or ballet slippers, but to really get the feel and look of a jazz dancer, it's fun to wear Capezio's Hermes sandals or jazz shoes. For the fun floor movements, and the transitions to and from them, you may be more comfortable if you remove your shoes.

Jazz pants, shown in the dance sequences, pages 118–131, can be worn too. They look good, and, more practically, they serve as a warming cover for leg muscles.

Music

Many of the songs played today have a peppy four-four beat that will set your mind, heart, and feet in motion. Some records and tapes that will help you plan and practice your routines are listed in each chapter. If one selection is unavailable, you can readily substitute it with another. A complete listing is given in the Appendix. Many of the old songs have been re-released on new labels by current recording stars. You can also find many "oldies but goodies" in thrift shops and at garage sales.

When you play a song, listen to the phrasing, the musical patterns, and the rhythms. Plan the jazz movements to "fit" the tune. If a phrase is repeated eight times at the beginning of a song, do one movement four times on your right side and four times on your left. Go on to another movement for the next phrase. This gives a dance variety and potential for improvisation. A wide range of music from Broadway show tunes, country and western, jazz, and rock should be used because the contrasting styles point out different ways to move and keep you from getting tired of the same beat.

How? How Much? How Often?

Before you begin limbering up, study the drawing that shows how your body works; you will be better able to understand the logical pattern designed for following the movements from head to toe. There is a reason for each movement. When you move only a shoulder, for example, you're

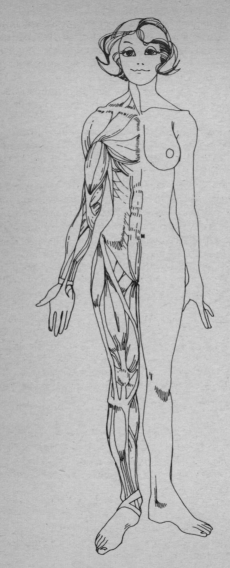

Drawing: Connie Williams.

also beginning to warm up your arm, and when you move your rib cage, your spine loosens.

Practice everything slowly and precisely at first, section by section, until you feel you are in control of that particular dance pattern and can do it smoothly without referring to the pictures. Practice in front of a mirror to compare your positions with the photographs.

How often should you jazzercise? As often as possible, but a thirty-minute session at least three times a week will do wonders for you. Try to move whenever the spirit hits you, because even five- and ten-minute spurts of movement will make you feel good! By the time you reach the routines in Chapter 8, you'll have all the basics at your fingertips, and you'll be dancing before you know it.

Let yourself go! It's not important if you don't look like a professional jazz dancer. Don't be too self-critical! Give yourself room to grow in your attitude toward yourself and your body. Be good to yourself by learning to become free and uninhibited in your movements! Let your body do the moving and your mind enjoy whatever it likes! Carly Simon says it best in her song *Attitude Dancing*.

The fantasies you may have about being a dancer will become reality! Whenever a band strikes up the music, you will smile, enjoy yourself, and show the world you're the jazziest dancer around.

How Your Body Works

Each part of your body is hinged to move in various ways. The exercises that follow will show you how to move your

Head: Side to side • Horizontally • Up and down • In a circle • In a swing

Shoulders: Up and down • Forward and back • Rotation

Arms and Elbows: Forward and back • Across your body and to the side • Swing • Circle • Flexion from the elbow

Hand and Wrist: Open and close your fingers • Circle and flexion from your wrist

Rib cage: Thrust forward, back, and side to side • Circle

Spine: Round • Flat • Arch • Straight • Twist

Pelvis: Forward • Back • Side to side • Circle • Lift

Leg—Thigh, Knee, and Shin: Forward • Back • Side to side laterally • Rotation from hip, knee

Foot and Ankle: Point • Flexion from ankle • Rotation • Lift onto ball of foot • Pull back onto heel

The bones are moved by muscles, which act like levers. There are flexor (bending) muscles and extensor (stretching) muscles. The muscle represents the power, the bone is the weight, and the joint is the point of support. Study the drawing to see how everything is connected and why it is important to warm up and use all your muscles for a total physical fitness program.

Suggested Schedule

Any type of body conditioning program, whether it is through dancing or a calisthenic-type workout, should consist of three parts: (1) the Warm-Up, (2) a Peak Work Period, and (3) a Cooling Down Period.

Beginners should devote more time to warming up than those who are used to exercising. After looking through the book, select two or three movement series from each chapter and set them to the following schedule. Choose those which are easiest for you to do at first, then add more as your endurance, strength, and flexibility increase. It is recommended that you exercise at least thirty minutes three times a week on nonconsecutive days.

The Warm-Up: Limbering and Loosening	10–12 minutes
Peak Work Period: A. Strength and Flexibility Body Brighteners Jazz Floor Fun	10 minutes
B. Cardiovascular Look, I'm Dancing	10 minutes
Cooling Down Period: Prop Positions Limbering and Loosening	8–10 minutes

As you begin to feel stronger and more energetic, and as the movements become easier, decrease the warm-up and cool-down time about five minutes each and increase the time spent on the Body Brighteners, Jazz Floor Fun, and Dancing.

It is important to pace yourself and to tune in to the reactions and feelings of your body. For example, if you feel very out of

14   JAZZERCISE

breath, with your heart beating rapidly, stop and take a few deep breaths. This will provide a short break and also revitalize your entire system with refreshing oxygen.

Everyone should be careful with such problem areas as lower backs, knees, elbows, and hips. Try not to strain by putting undue pressures on those areas.

A beginner will almost always experience some muscle soreness at first. This is due to metabolic waste (lactic acid), which remains in the muscle after exercising. Do some additional stretching to help alleviate the soreness. A warm bath is also very soothing.

3 Limbering and Loosening

Now that you know the practical aspects of jazzercise, you're ready to begin loosening, limbering, and getting your body in condition to do the jazz exercises and movements.

Limbering up is a logical, healthy, and professional process because it utilizes specific parts of the body, and the space around it, in a full range of motion. It will help you move and dance better because it puts you in complete control of your body and gives you a better sense of body alignment.

Start with the first section of this chapter, the Warm-Up, and soon you will be supplying a greater flow of oxygen to your lungs, increasing your heart rate, and loosening the tightness of your muscles. A gradual toning (conditioning) of them will occur as you stretch (elongate) and contract (tighten) in opposing movements—right to left, up and down, forward and backward. All of this is necessary to prepare your body to do more strenuous and demanding dance patterns.

Most of us picture ourselves in a rigid, limited sense without realizing that we are actually able to discipline our bodies so that we can move each part separately, section by section (see illustration, page 12). These movements, which are called Isolations, follow the Warm-Up. You will learn to "isolate" rib cage from waist, shoulder from arm. As you proceed from picture to picture, you will discover that you are moving from the head to the shoulders, to the hands, to the arms, to the rib cage, to the hips, to the spine in a logical, page-by-page progression.

Jazz Pliés are next. They move the legs in a series of bends that use both the traditional ballet foot placements and a jazz foot placement. In ballet positions, you place your feet in a "turned-out" fashion, while in jazz positions, your feet are placed in a parallel "no turn-out" manner. Jazz Pliés are a syncopated, rhythmic pattern of easy bending and stretching. The movements lead from one to the next subtly and gently.

Always try to do each exercise in this chapter at least eight times unless otherwise specified.

Now to get you started on the right foot—and the left foot too—turn on the music! Any peppy tune with a percussive four-four beat will do. Limber and loosen to The Temptations's

"Papa Was a Rollin' Stone," "Heartbeat" by War, or "Black Frost" by Grover Washington!

Smile, and don't forget to use your mirror! It can be a good friend as it helps you compare your positions with those pictured and reflects your new, slim and trim shape.

THE WARM-UP

The Warm-Up is in three parts: Ready, Set, Go! Its opposing stretches move vertically and laterally. They are designed to put your body in a delicate, delightful balance and to prepare it for the many marvelous movements that follow. It's a quick way to get rolling!

Ready . . .

A. Begin the Warm-Up by stretching your right arm overhead and lifting your rib cage. Bend your right knee forward and stretch your left leg back. Feet flat on the floor.

B. Repeat on your left side.

C. Swing both arms to the back and bend at your waist.

D. Swing both arms up and lift them overhead. Keep your feet flat on the floor.

Repeat these movements at least four times. Stretch tall. Think happy thoughts.

. . . Set . . .

Now . . . *stretch* laterally.

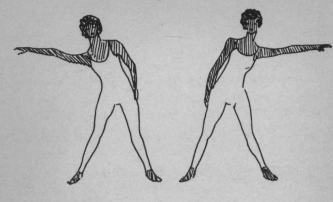

A. Feet apart. Stretch your right arm to the right, pulling your rib cage as far as you can to the right. Your left arm is down.

B. Reverse the movement to the left; really pull that arm and rib cage out, out, out.

C. Bend both knees and swing both arms energetically over to the right.

D. And do it the other way—to the left—and straighten both knees.

E. & F. Now bend both knees and swing your arms back to the right and straighten both knees.

. . . Go!

G. Feet close together. Bend both knees and touch the floor with your hands. Then . . .

H. . . . stretch until you think you can touch the sky.

Four times for each of these and you're ready to dance, to feel the music, to Go! It's JAZZ!

ISOLATIONS

To "isolate" means to work each part of your body independently. It may take concentration initially, but once you get your thoughts and your muscles working together, you'll reacquaint yourself with your body, and you'll know it's the way to go for the ultimate in movement. Let's discover how it works. Begin with . . .

The Head

YES

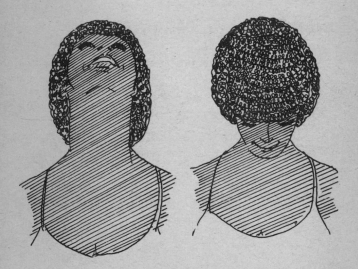

A. Stand straight and tall. Drop your head back . . .

B. . . . and forward as if to say, "Yes," I can do it!

Repeat four times.

JAZZERCISE

NO

C. Turn your head to the right, pause, and pull.

D. Turn your head to the left, pause, and pull as if to say, "No," I can't stop, because it feels great.

Repeat four times.

MAYBE

E. Tilt your head to the right . . .

F. . . . and to the left for a "Maybe."

Four times please.

HEAD SWING

A. Begin from a heads-up position, then tilt your head up and to the right.

B. Slowly begin the downward swing . . .

C. . . . until your chin is to your chest. Continue the circular swing around to the left and up. Reverse direction, swing down and up again to the right.

The rhythm is: swing right to left, back and forth.

JAZZERCISE

PAGODA SQUARE

A. Stand straight and tall. Clasp your hands over your head. Lift your head out of your neck and push your right ear to your right elbow. Keep your head straight forward; do not tilt.

B. Do the same to the other side. Back and forth.

C. Front—thrust your chin forward.

D. Back—make a double chin.

Remember! Do the square four times.

Shoulder Isolations

FORWARD-BACK

A. Standing straight and tall, push your right shoulder forward . . .

B. . . . push it up . . .

C. . . . pull it back, and repeat with your left shoulder.

SHOULDER ROLL

A. Rotate your right shoulder forward . . .

B. . . . up . . .

C. . . . and back. Repeat with your left shoulder.

Give the movement a "come hither flavor" so you'll be ready to use it in the dance. Remember, it's got to *move* and roll fluidly.

SHOULDER BLADE PUSH

A. Stand tall, feet apart, arms forward at a 45° angle. Pull your right shoulder blade back. If it doesn't work, concentrate on just your shoulder blade or only your arm will move. You want to feel it in your back. Let go.

B. Pull your left blade back. Let go.

C. Pull both blades back together. Hold it four beats! Let go!

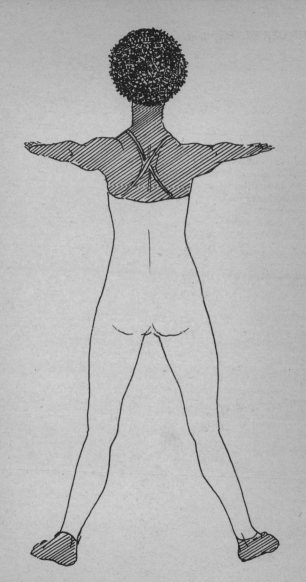

D. Your goal? Loosen up your muscles, limber up, and try to make the blades touch. They can't, but it's good to try.

LIMBERING AND LOOSENING 29

Hand Isolations

JAZZ HANDS

Jazz Hands are strong! They beat to the music, sometimes they carry a rhythm all their own while the body rests. So let's loosen up the fingers and the knuckles until you feel the energy flow through your arms and into your hands.

A. Stand with your feet apart. Tighten both fists in front of your abdomen, squeeze them, and tighten all your arm and hand muscles.

B. Quickly open up your arms and fingers.

C. Clench your fists again out to the side.

D. And explode your hands out in front.

Repeat the sequence energetically and enthusiastically.

FINGER SQUEEZE

Your hands will feel limber and loose as you touch each finger to your thumb and squeeze. Do it with your right hand, your left hand, and then both hands together.

Touch your index finger to thumb and squeeze together. Follow through using your middle finger squeezed to thumb; your ring finger squeezed to thumb; your little finger squeezed to thumb.

PUTTING IT TOGETHER

A. Stretch your left arm long—out to the left side.

B. Bend your elbow and pull your hand to your shoulder.

C. Lift your elbow up and drop your hand down with its back facing forward.

D. Straighten your arm and stretch your hand out to the side . . . with a strong burst of energy—Jazz Hand.

Do it with your left arm, your right, and both together. This is a basic arm-hand movement which can be used in dance routines.

Rib Cage Isolations

The first time you try to isolate your rib cage, it may seem awkward, but think of your rib cage as being hinged at your waist and at the top of your chest. To move it, you must concentrate on it. It's worth every effort because it tightens up your midriff quickly. Begin with your body straight, feet apart.

SIDE TO SIDE

A. Stretch your arms out to the side. Reach out to the right with your right arm and slide your rib cage to the right. pulling your ribs away from your waist. Pretend that someone is pushing your rib cage from the left to the right until you loosen up.

B. Try it to the left. Reach out to the left with your left arm and your rib cage will actually glide over to the other side as though you were being pushed from the right.

FORWARD-BACK

C. Push your rib cage forward . . .

D. . . . and back as though someone is punching you in the tummy.

RIB CAGE SQUARE

A. Place your hands on your pelvic bones—push your rib cage forward.

B. Slide it right.

C. Push your rib cage back.

D. Slide it left . . . until you can feel yourself moving it in a square. Also rotate it in a smooth circle.

Hip Isolations

The hips, like the rib cage, are hinged in two places: at the waist and at the hip socket. They are easy to isolate, especially when you're moving them to the beat of a good song. It's not like old-fashioned exercise; it's up-to-date jazzercise, and you'll love the feel of it! You'll lose inches around your waist and hips while preparing yourself for more advanced dance movements.

SIDE TO SIDE

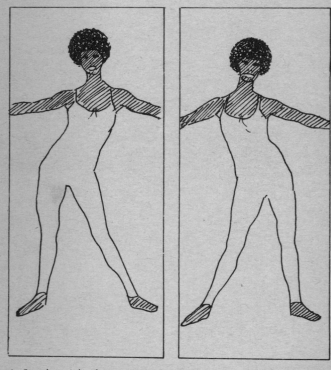

A. Stand straight, feet apart, and with your knees locked and arms to the side. Thrust your right hip out to the right.

B. Thrust your left hip out to the left.

FORWARD-BACK

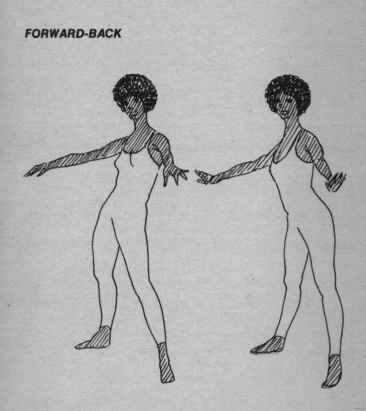

A. Thrust your pelvis forward.   B. Thrust your pelvis to the back.

Remember to repeat all these movements at least eight times.

A. *Feet apart*. Now with your *knees bent* slightly, thrust your right hip to the right.

B. Thrust your left hip to the left.

HIP SQUARE #1

Note: Knees are bent, feet are apart. When the knees are bent, the hips move even more easily than when the knees are locked.

C. Push your pelvis back . . .

D. . . . and forward.

A. *Feet together, knees bent,* thrust your right hip to the right.

B. Thrust your left hip to the left.

HIP SQUARE #2

Note: Knees are bent, feet together.

This second version of the Hip Square uses a different foot position. Notice that it's a bit more difficult to isolate the hips when the feet are together. Each version offers an expressive opportunity to move differently with the music.

C. Push your pelvis back.

D. Push your pelvis forward.

HIP LIFT

With several beginning hip movements literally under your belt, let's step into a Hip Lift movement to go with those you already know. See how quickly you can begin to dance? Snap into each position with lots of energy! This Hip Lift is a typical jazz movement.

A. Begin by standing tall, feet together. Smile. Feel the mood of the music.

B. Thrust your hip to the right, lift your right leg and touch your toe to the front. Let your whole body follow through with a fluid motion. Swing to the right and return to the beginning position.

C. Repeat the same thrust, leg lift, and toe touch to the left while your body swings through. Return to the basic front position. The rhythm is snappy as you thrust right and back. Thrust left and back. Pick up the four-four time and feel the beat echoing in your movements!

HIP WALK

The Hip Walk is often interjected throughout a jazz dance. Learn to do it rhythmically as you move forward, backward, or in a circle.

A. Begin with the basic Hip Lift position. Thrust your right hip to the right as you step forward on your right foot and dip your body slightly with your knees slightly bent.

B. Step forward on your left foot and thrust your left hip to the left, placing your left foot forward and dipping your body slightly. Continue walking forward until you get the feel of the movement. Then, with the music, move around the room, anywhere. Do it with soul! Make it funky!

Spine Tinglers

You'll enjoy the feeling of loosening up the tension in a tight back by exercising the spinal column. The lumbar, that lower back which sometimes causes stiffness, can become as supple as a rag doll. It may take a little practice to move through round, flat, straight, and arched positions—the spine may be more difficult to manipulate than the hips—but it can be done. *Never* begin with spine exercises. ALWAYS BE SURE to do spine isolations only after you feel adequately limbered. So keep the music going and try it!

A. From a stand tall, feet apart position, bend from your hips and drop your arms to the floor, knees straight. *Round* and relax your back.

B. Lift your chest so it's parallel to the floor, arms extended out, and your back *flat* as a tabletop. Tighten your abdominal muscles. (Check yourself in the mirror to be sure your spine is flat.) Keep trying; it takes practice!

JAZZERCISE

C. Straighten your arms up overhead and think of pulling your spinal column *straight*.

D. *Arch* your back slowly and bend your arms back and out to the side. Hold for a beat or two. Repeat from position A until you feel all tensions escaping from your back like steam from a tea kettle.

ANOTHER GOOD SPINE TINGLER

A. Beginning from the flat tabletop back position, . . .

B. . . . round your back and *pull* your tummy in tight as if you were trying to touch it to your spine. Relax your tummy and return to the tabletop back position. Do this movement at least eight times.

JAZZ PLIÉS (BENDS)

Plié (ple-a) is the French word for "bend." Each series of Pliés is done with the feet in different positions. They are excellent for warming up the legs and feet. They stretch the muscles and tighten up the thighs. The torso and spine have to be straight. It is important to keep your knees over your toes; do not turn them in knock-knee fashion. If you do the movements to a jazzy beat, they are as much fun to do as they are good for you.

Turned Out Pliés

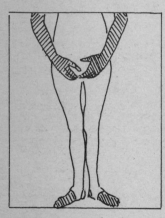

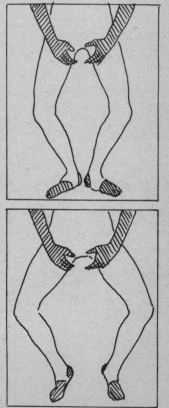

A. *First* Position: Heels together, toes out.

B. Bend your knees slightly. Your heels should not release from the floor.

C. Now lift your heels up from the floor and balance on your toes.

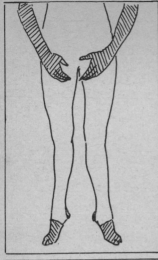

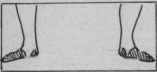

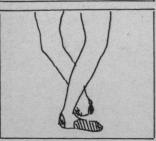

D. Straighten your knees, still balancing on your toes. Drop your heels and return to First Position.

Think of the rhythm as bend (1), lift (2), straighten (3), drop (4), as you count to a four-beat measure of the music.

E. *Second* Position: Feet apart, heels in, toes out. Repeat the rhythm in the Second Position: bend your knees slightly, lift your heels, straighten your knees, drop your heels.

F. *Fourth* Position: Your right foot is behind with your heel in, toe out. Your left foot is about eight inches in front of your right heel. Repeat bend, lift, straighten, and drop in this position.

G. *Fifth* Position: Your left heel and right toe are together. Bend, lift, straighten, and drop.

Note: Do each sequence four times in each position. *Third* position is not included in this series because it is seldom used.

No Turn Out Pliés

In the previous positions, the feet are turned out. In the No Turn Out position, the feet are parallel. In each position, repeat the same movements: bend, lift, straighten, drop.

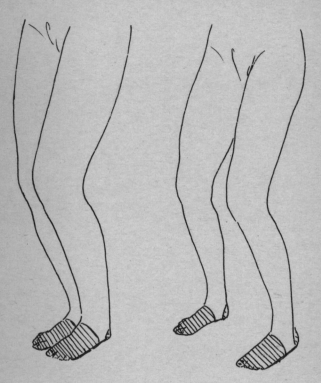

A. *First* Position: Parallel feet, feet together. Bend, lift, straighten, and drop. Repeat four times.

B. *Second* Position: Your feet are parallel but separated. Do the same movements: bend, lift, straighten, and drop four times.

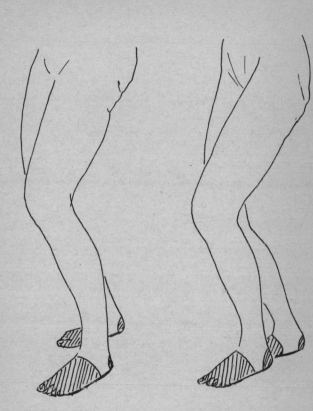

C. *Fourth* Position: Feet are parallel but now your left foot is slightly in front of your right foot. Repeat the movements.

D. *Fifth* Position: Your feet are parallel but your left heel is placed next to your right toe and the positions are repeated with rhythmical feeling.

4   *Body Brighteners*

Nikki Miller (left) and Marsha Mayer combine several of the movements shown in the Body Brighteners.

With your body feeling all loose and limber, it is time to turn to more serious demands. You'll be "mini-dancing" as you combine each series of exercises to form short routines. Use tunes such as "Sunshine on My Shoulder" or "Willie and the Hand Jive." Music by Scott Joplin or The Jazz Crusaders also provides a bouncy background.

The Body Brighteners utilize the Isolations you learned in Chapter 3, then they take you giant steps farther by offering a wider range of exercise combinations. The Top Torso Tighteners will tone your chest, shoulders, arms, and upper back. The Middle Modifiers will slim your waist and midriff. The Thigh Thinners will stretch and firm your thighs and hips and strengthen your legs so that they will carry you wherever you might wander.

Your body will feel alert and awake, you'll meet each day with refreshed energy when you make the Body Brighteners a regular part of your exercise schedule. They'll make you feel good about yourself, knowing you can meet almost any challenge the day may have in store for you.

Please remember to repeat each exercise series at least eight times unless the directions state differently.

TOP TORSO TIGHTENERS

Elbow Thrust Stretch

Think of this movement as accenting each beat of the music. Make your moves strong and definite. Begin in a relaxed standing position, arms down at your sides.

A. Bring your right hand close to your right shoulder.

B. Cross your right elbow in front of your chest, hand still close to your shoulder.

C. Pull your elbow back and to the side and turn your hand over, palm up.

D. Push your hand straight out to the side and flex your hand upward at the wrist.

Repeat with your left arm and then work both hands together. Really push your arms out, accentuating each movement with the beat of the music.

Elbow Square

This exercise will eliminate underarm flab. It's a posture pleaser also.

A. Clasp your arm in front of your chest.

B. Lift arms overhead.

C. Drop your arms down to your abdomen.

D. Twist your arms and upper torso to the right then swing them to the left, repeating at least four times.

Single Triangle

More Torso Tighteners which will strengthen your upper back and release tension in your shoulders. They are effective, especially if you've been sitting or standing in one place for a long time.

A. Stretch your right arm overhead.

B. Bend your right elbow behind your head and touch your right fingertips to your left shoulder at least eight times. Repeat with your left arm.

Double Triangle

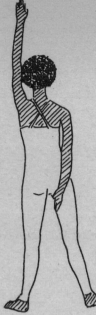

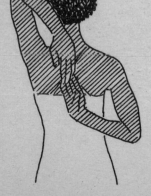

A. Stretch your left arm overhead and your right arm down and slightly behind your back.

B. Bend both elbows and try to touch the fingertips of both hands together in the middle of your back. You'll really have to practice, *stretch* . . .

Reverse and repeat to get the same stretch on the other side.

Elbow Touch

A. Touch both hands to your shoulders.

B. Swing your elbows in front of your chest until they touch. Return to the beginning position and repeat about ten times.

C. You can observe how the middle back area stretches into a smooth line. This movement eliminates any excess flabbiness around tight straps that may ruin the smoothness of your clothes.

Wings

A. Bend slightly forward from your waist and keep your back flat (as in the flat back isolation, page 40). Stretch your arms out to the side.

B. By bending your hands into the side of your body, your elbows will bend to simulate the look of wings. Repeat it quickly and sharply. Tensions will fly from your back and shoulder area!

Hand Jive

Here's a movement you'll love to do. The song "Willie and the Hand Jive" is the perfect accompaniment. The rhythm is: bounce-stretch. Bend and straighten your knees while opening and closing your hands. See Routine 46, page 171.

A. Feet together, arms extended in front of your chest, fists clenched.

B. Straighten your knees, and stretch your fingers into Jazz Hands position.

C. Arms overhead, fists clenched, bounce down.

D. Stretch up, hands open.

E. Arms out to side, fists clenched, knees bent, bounce down.

F. Stretch out, hands open.

G. Bend from hips, flat back, arms back, fists clenched. Bounce down.

H. Stretch out, hands open.

Repeat the Hand Jive sequence at least ten times.

MIDDLE MODIFIERS

As the name implies, the following sequences are designed to swish away excess inches around the middle.

Midriff Minimizer #1

A. Stand with feet apart and hands clasped behind your back.

B. Twist from your waist to the right and swing your hands around to your left side . . .

C. . . . and to the right—to and fro, fast and slow.

Midriff Minimizer #2

A. With your feet apart now, clasp your hands in front of your chest . . .

B. . . . and swing them to the right side, back, and down as you twist from your waist . . .

C. . . . and up over your head.

Let the momentum of the swing carry your arms to the left side and swing directly into the same movements on that side. Continue swinging around and over from one side to the other several times. Swing and sway your waist away!

Midriff Minimizer #3

A. Stand tall, well poised, with your arms crossed in front of your chest. Hesitate with a beat between, then . . .

B. . . . let go and let your energy flow. Bend your knees and swing out, first to the right, then to the left, returning to the sophisticated pose in between. It's two moods of you.

Waistline Stretcher

A. Stand with your feet apart and flat on the floor, your hands reaching up and away.

B. Bend left from your waist; feel the stretch on the right, the crunch on the left.

C. Twist, flatten your back, pull your tummy muscles tight, and reach out to the side as far as you can. Reach, reach.

D. Slowly, and with control, drop your body over your left knee and clasp your ankle with your hands and hold.

Return to the stretch position and repeat on the other side. This is a beautiful rhythmic exercise that is a joy to do.

BODY BRIGHTENERS

Jazz Strut

The following series of exercises is particularly good for firming the lower abdominal area. Select an up-tempo tune, such as "Your Mama Don't Dance," and combine the Strut and the Lean (opposite page) in a mini-routine.

A. Hands on hips, lift your right knee to chest level. Point that right toe strongly.

B. Step together, bring your right foot to meet the left, and bend forward from your hips with your back straight.

Pick up your left leg, point the toe, straighten up, and you're in position to do the other side. This is a stylized march done as though you were strutting in a parade—the eyes of the audience upon you.

Jazz Lean

A. Begin with your feet together, then put your right foot forward with its heel tapping the floor. Lean back, arms bent back in Jazz Hands style as if to say, "Look at me!"

B. Step back, bringing your left foot together with the right. Bend forward from your hips, flat back, swinging your arms back as you bend.

Repeat with your left foot forward. Alternate right and left, leaning and bending rhythmically to the beat of the music.

THIGH THINNERS

Crazy Pliés #1

You've already warmed up with the Jazz Pliés (pages 42–45), now you can have more fun with these crazy variations. Let go of all your inhibitions. Try them with Ringo Starr's "Occapella" or Scott Joplin's "The Cascades."

A. Feet apart, hands on shoulders, elbows pointed out to the side.

B. Bend both knees . . .

C. . . . and lean over to your right and touch your right elbow to your right knee.

D. Bend deeper, bring your body to the center, and touch both elbows to both knees.

E. Stand up straight and tall, stretching your legs. Your elbows are bent to the sides and your hands are back in position to repeat the sequence on the left side.

Crazy Pliés #2

A. Feet apart, your toes turned in. Bend forward from your hips and keep your back straight. Your hands are behind your back.

B. Bend your knees together and touch them in knock-knee fashion. Straighten up. Repeat several times.

Crazy Pliés #3

A. Feet together, knees bent, hands on knees, leaning over.

B. First step your right foot out to the right side, then step your left foot to the left, resulting in a wide stance. Step your right foot back to center, then your left foot to center, thus returning to the beginning position. Repeat, moving the feet alternately out, out, in, in.

Crazy Pliés #4

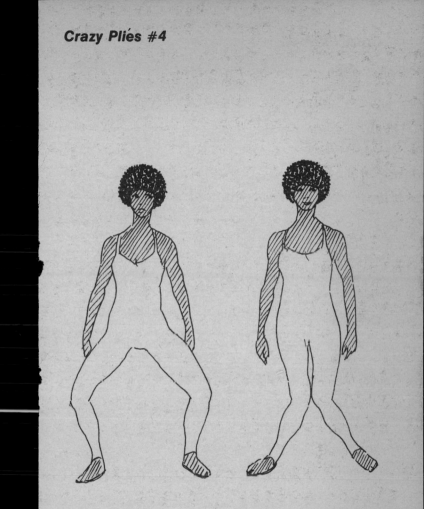

A. Feet apart, knees bent, hands at sides, back straight.

B. Knock knees together, then open them apart. Do this in a quick *in-out* movement with the *in* movement *accented*.

You can combine these Crazy Pliés for a fun routine by themselves or use them as a theme for a longer dance arrangement. Be creative! Remember, you're terrific!

Leg Fly-Aways

Leg Fly-Aways are beautifully choreographed to lilting tempos such as Janis Ian's "At Seventeen" and Tim Weisberg's "Listen to the City." Between each movement, you return to the basic poised stance shown in position A. The rhythm is: A-B-A, C-A, D-A.

FRONT

A. Begin with the basic poised stance.

B. Point your left foot to the left side and open your arms as shown. Return to the poised stance.

C. Bend your right knee in a deep lunge and place your left leg out to the left side in a long stretch. Return to the poised stance.

D. Lift your left leg up and out to the side. Return to the poised stance. Repeat all the movements on your right side.

BACK

A. Poised stance.

B. Point your left foot behind you, swing your arms back with your leg, lean forward. Return to the poised stance.

C. Lunge your left leg behind you in a deep bend, touching your hands to the floor in front of you. Return to the poised stance.

D. Swing your left leg up and away to the back. Return to the poised stance. Repeat the movements with your right leg.

Much of the visual excitement of watching a professional jazz performance is the total movement involved. The dancers deftly and purposely create a change of pace by alternating from an upright to a floor position many times. Touching the floor, performing on it, and rising again are accomplished smoothly, gracefully, subtly, and seemingly without effort.

It's an appearance that takes effort, thought, and practice. But with it all are the benefits of additional limbering and loosening. Four different ways to descend to the floor are shown in this chapter. While you're on the floor, there are more exercises that are good to do and good for you. You'll learn how to stand up again too, without a pause, using fluid-like movements.

You may discover that many of the exercises on the floor are as much fun, perhaps more, as those done while standing. Why? Because gravity exerts a tremendous pull on the body at all times, but its effects are milder when you are positioned on the floor; you are not working against your total body weight. The heart rate is not as easily raised, and you will not feel as out of breath as you may when you are jumping and hopping.

Think of the floor as a stage, an unexplored dimension, with you as the center of the entire space around your body. Try new movements and swing to the music. Bounce against the floor, roll on it, let it work as a massage against the various parts of your body. You'll feel a new sense of body placement, alignment, and flexibility.

For jazz floor fun exercises, wear soft shoes or remove your shoes. You can work out on any floor that is convenient—carpeted or bare. An exercise mat can be used to cushion your body.

Repeat each movement at least eight times, four times to the right and four times to the left unless otherwise specified.

DOWN TO THE FLOOR

The following movements are designed to take your body from a standing to a floor position without effort. Each one will stretch your legs and body and make you feel graceful and well balanced.

Descent #1

A. Stand tall with your arms over-head, feet together.

B. Gracefully lower yourself, placing your left knee on the floor.

C. Then place your right knee next to your left.

D. Shift your weight to the left and smoothly sit down. (Do not plunk.)

Descent #2

A. Lunge to your left and bend your left knee.

B. Lunge more deeply and place your hands on the floor.

C. Pivot to the right as you place one hand on each side of your right leg.

D. Slowly slide your right leg forward and place your left knee on the floor. You can follow this with the Jazz Split movement sequence on pages 92–93.

Descent #3

This one will lead you into the Jazz Twist position (pages 86–87).

A. From the standing, arm stretched overhead position, cross your right foot about two feet behind your left foot.

B. Drop your body so that your right knee is on the floor next to the left side of your left foot.

C. With your knee and foot still in the same position, drop your body so that you are sitting on the floor. At the same time, follow the movement through and bring your arms down to just below your shoulder.

Descent #4

A. From the feet together, flat back position, extend both arms forward.

B. Place your hands on the floor far out in front of your feet.

C. Walk your hands forward, dropping your hips so your torso is straight . . .

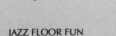

D. . . . and relax. From this last descent, you can easily move into the following sequence of floor movements.

FOUR CORNERS

Follow these vigorously and enthusiastically for a thinner derrière. Do each exercise once, using your right then left leg, then go on to the next . . . and the next. Come back and begin again . . . and again. You will have an entire floor routine that will hold your interest during all your jazzercise sessions.

Upside-Down V

A. Place your knees together and your arms straight.

B. Spread your feet and curl your toes under.

C. Stretch your legs and lock your knees as tightly as possible, hold for two beats of the music, and return to the beginning position above. Repeat and/or proceed to the next movement.

Lean Away

A. Sit on your heels with your knees together, arms stretched forward.

B. Extend your left leg straight back and point your toe.

C. Lift your hips and shift your weight to your right hip.

D. Continue the shift in a smooth fashion, moving up and over until you can place both hips on the floor. Touch the floor with your left elbow so that you feel a good stretch on your inner thigh. Be sure to repeat this on both sides. You don't want to be lopsided!

Leg Cross-Swing

The gluteus-maximus muscles, located in the derriere, will be used fully when you do this movement sequence with your body weight supported by your elbows. It may seem a strange position, but the more you move in different ways, the more you will tighten and tone your muscles.

A. Knees together, elbows down, hands clasped, . . .

B. . . . extend your left leg to the left side and point your toe; tighten your knee.

C. Cross your left leg over your right leg and swing it far back and to the side, keeping your toe pointed.

76

D. From the cross-over position, extend the same leg as high as possible toward the ceiling. Return to the starting position. Repeat with the same leg four times, then reverse the movement, using the other leg.

The Up-Lift

You'll be sure to feel the wonderful "up-lifting" effects of this exercise. Each lift works on the derriere, the tummy, and the upper arms.

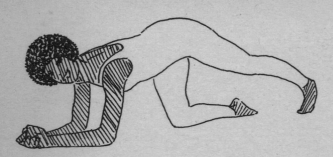

A. Start with the basic position shown for the Leg Cross-Swing on page 76 and stretch your left leg straight back and curl your toe under.

B. Stretch your right leg in line with your left leg so your entire body is straight and parallel with the floor.

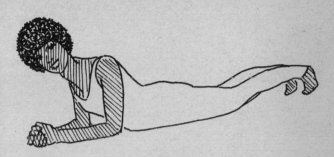

C. Drop your tummy to the floor and relax for a second, then . . .

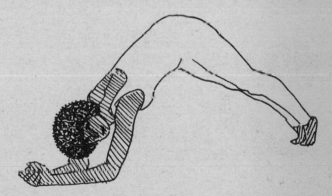

D. . . . with a burst of energy, lift your derriere into the air. Repeat C and D a few times until you can do it with vim and vigor.

This is the end of one floor fun sequence. So flip back to page 74 and begin again with the Upside-Down V and follow through. Always do each movement on each side of the body several times before proceeding to the following movement. Try these movements to Neil Sedaka's "Nana's Song" or "You Are the Sunshine of My Life" by Stevie Wonder.

INDIAN CROSS

The previous movements were designed to firm your derrière. Those which follow will eliminate excess inches you may have below your waistline, on the back, and along the outer thigh. They tighten and tone you so beautifully, you'll have a new aura of confidence; you'll know you look great in everything you wear!

 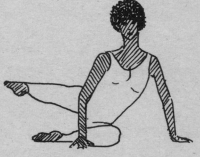

A. This is known as the Indian Cross (or Swastika) position. Your left leg is bent in front of you, the right bent in the same way but positioned slightly to the back.

B. Lift your right leg as high off the floor as possible and support your weight on your hands in front of you.

C. Put your right leg back into the beginning position, swing your left arm over your head and to the side as you slide your right hand on the floor and to the side for support. Put all the energy you can into this movement and you should feel a good stretch along the left side of your body.

D. Now swing both arms up and over to the other side until you feel the same vigorous stretch.

E. Lift your right leg from the floor, straightening it and pointing your toe.

F. With an extra bit of effort, lift your hips from the floor, straighten your arm, and kick your leg to the side. Continue with the movements that follow in an uninterrupted dance pattern.

(continued on next page)

G. Place your left hip back on the floor and at the same time bring your right knee toward your chest, clench your fist, and bring your elbow down toward your thigh.

H. Stretch your right leg back and right arm forward.

I. Return to the basic Indian Cross position but swing your arms to the left, leaning back with your weight on your right hip.

J. Lean to the floor, bend your elbows, and raise your right leg high off the floor, keeping your head down. This is fun to do and adds variety to the movement. Return to the basic Indian Cross position, then flow into the movements on the next page.

INDIAN CROSS CIRCLE

This is the prettiest and most graceful of the Indian Cross movements.

A. Drop your chest over your left knee with your arms extended out at your sides and your head downward.

B. Lift your head and pull your chest up with it.

C. Begin to twist your upper torso to the right . . .

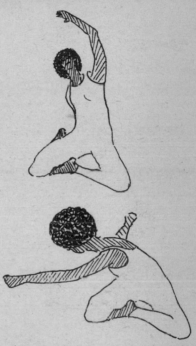

D. . . . and accentuate the twist.

E. Slide your right elbow to the floor, lean back, and slightly arch your upper body. Swing your left arm up, around, and over your head as though you are drawing a circle in the air. Circle back and through the sequence, in reverse, and return to Position A.

Repeat the sequence beginning from the top of page 80 on the left side of your body, gliding effortlessly from one side to the other. Select any section of these movements which you like and repeat them time and again. Use Billy Preston's "I Wrote a Simple Song" for rhythmic inspiration.

JAZZ TWIST

Now the back of your upper thigh will receive the special attention it needs to prevent unsightly "saddle bags."

A. Sit on your right hip, with your right knee bent. Cross your left foot over your right knee. Squeeze your left knee to your chest with your right arm. Your left hand is on the floor behind you, supporting your body weight.

B. Let go of your leg, put both hands on the floor behind you, and lean back slightly. Kick your left leg up and out.

C. Cross your left leg over your right knee in a swinging motion; lean forward and swing your arms up and back.

D. Lift your upper body and swing your arms up over your head on an upbeat of the music.

JAZZ LEG STRETCHES

By stretching your legs, you'll be able to kick higher and look jazzier. Those Body Brightening Leg Fly-Aways will seem less difficult because of it too. Soon you'll be jazz dancing—kicking, leaping, jumping, and scooting across the floor. Your legs will have the long and elastic look of Juliet Prowse or Rudolf Nureyev. The bouncy benefits will spill over into your everyday life as well, making it easier to tackle the flights of stairs in your office building, or to lift those heavy grocery bags. All in all, you'll get more of a "kick" out of life! So now put on Mark-Almond's "The City" and start to stretch!

Floor Lunge

A. Stretch out your right leg, bend your left knee so your foot touches your right upper thigh.

B. Swing your right arm up and over your head.

C. Pull your upper torso up out of your hips as you stretch forward over your left knee and follow through to the floor. Come back up, reversing your movements until you are again in the first position. Repeat four times; each time, try to stretch a little farther forward and down. Then switch your leg position, left leg out, and so forth, and repeat on the left side.

Cross-Over Lift

A. Stretch your left leg to the side. Cross your right leg over the left and place your right foot on the floor in front of your left thigh. Support your body weight on both hands.

B. Touch your right elbow to the floor.

C. Swing your right arm up and over to the left.

D. Lift your hips up and stretch your left leg and your right arm in opposition to each other as far as they will go; really pull until you are balanced. Now you have found your center of gravity.

E. Drop your body and return to the first position.

F. Lift your left leg about twelve inches from the floor, stretching the muscles on the inner thigh. Drop your leg to the floor. Repeat the sequence on both sides of your body several times.

Jazz Split

The Jazz Split is one of the basic floor positions in jazz dance. Many of the movements you have already done work together with this basic position. It's also a marvelous stretch for the inner and outer thigh. It prepares you for the ultimate—the ability to do a full split. Looking at the pictures, begin at the bottom of the page and move upward then back down—A to D, D to A.

A. Stretch your right leg forward at about a 45° angle to your body. Bend your left knee as far back as you can. Stretch your left arm forward and your right arm back with your head down.

B. Lift your head and chest and arms slightly.

C. Continue the lift; lean gently backward until you can place your right hand on the floor.

D. Continue leaning backward until your elbow is on the floor; lift your left arm up and over your head in a circle.

Reverse the pattern. Your body should flow back and forth while your arm carries the flow of the motion.

Long-Leg Super Stretch

This stretch will make your stride longer and the feel of it lighter. It's an especially good and effective stretch for the inner thighs. Between each stretch shown, return to the first "knees bent" position.

A. Begin with both knees bent, legs apart, feet flat on the floor, and your hands holding your ankles.

B. Stretch your right leg out to the side until your knee locks, stretching your body over your leg as you go. Bring your leg back to the beginning position.

C. Stretch your left leg out to the side and return to the beginning position.

D. Stretch both legs out to the side simultaneously and lean your chest forward. Back to the beginning position.

E. Lift your right leg high, pulling it up by your ankle. Pull, stretch, give it all you've got!

F. Swing the leg across your body and over to your left knee and hold. Return to the basic position and repeat the routine with your left leg.

Remember to repeat the entire sequence eight times.

LONG SIT SWINGS

These are jazzy, swingy ways to tone up your tummy. They're fun to do in rhythmic patterns with songs like Jim Croce's "Bad, Bad Leroy Brown" or the "Theme from 'S.W.A.T.'"

Swing Under

A. Stretch both legs straight in front of you. Reach your hands forward as though you were trying to touch the floor.

B. Bend your knees. Swing your legs up and clap your hands under your knees.

Repeat this swing in time to the music for an entire phrasing.

Sit-Up Swing

A. Beginning from (or following through from) the Swing Under position (top of page 96), round your back, bend your knees into your chest, and place your feet flat on the floor. Clasp your hands tightly around your knees, inhale through your nose, and really tense your muscles.

B. Exhale through your nose, drop down to the floor, and shoot your arms back and your legs forward.

C. Sit up to the rounded, contracted position A, inhale through your nose, then . . .

D. . . . stretch your legs out forward, pull your arms up over your head, pulling your spine straight in a final stretch. Think of this as a rhythmic repetition of in, out, in, up.

Swinging Shoulder Stand

This is a movement which rolls from the floor backward and up onto your shoulders. When you do this correctly, you'll feel like an Olympic gymnast in a tumbling routine. And, as an added bonus, it will flatten your tummy and strengthen your upper and middle back.

A. Sit up straight with your legs forward, toes pointed, and your arms relaxed at your sides.

B. Roll back slowly, bend your knees, and lift your legs from the floor.

C. Let the swing carry your body farther back up onto your shoulders, knees still bent.

D. As you balance on your shoulders, extend your legs upward and hold. Roll back down gracefully and slowly, with control, to the beginning position. Repeat as often as you like.

CRAZY ROCK AND ROLLS

It's fun to put these rollin' movements to the rockin' music of the fifties. "Boogie-beat" music, together with rhythmic rollers, is a crazy combination that makes you feel like grooving and grinning. If only Bill Haley could see you "Shake, Rattle and Roll" to his "(We're Gonna) Rock Around the Clock" and "Rock-A-Beatin' Boogie"!!!

Unique movements such as these will work more magic on your hips, tummy, and thighs than any electrical exercise rolling machine ever could. So put some soul into your rollin' and rock out!

Roll-Over #1

A. Legs apart, feet flat on the floor, knees bent, lean on your hands behind you.

B. Swing your left hand to your right toe.

C. Roll over to the left and touch your right knee to the floor.

Return to the beginning position and repeat the sequence on the other side. Alternate rolling to the right and to the left ten times.

Roll-Over #2

A. Now stretch your legs apart, hands back and flat on the floor.

B. Touch your left hand to your right toe.

C. *Roll* down to the floor onto your back. Lift your right leg high up and . . .

D. . . . swing your leg over to your left side and touch the floor with your toe, then roll back up to the beginning position.

Repeat the roll on the other side. The rhythm is: touch, roll, swing, return. Reverse sides. The swing of your leg will put you into motion and carry you from one side to the other.

Bumper Thumpers

Bumper thumpers are constant rolling motions using the legs in different patterns. Each time you change the leg movement, continue the rolling rhythmically without stopping. Have fun "bumping" and "thumping" with one of the rock and roll songs mentioned on page 100.

This Basic Floor Roll position will be used for the rolls on the following pages. Sit tall and stretch your legs forward . . . take a deep breath, smile, and . . . go.

A. Roll onto your left hip. Support your body with your left hand on the floor at your side. Roll over to your right side. Continue back and forth several times, feeling the fun of rolling to the beat.

B. Rolling onto your left hip again, swing your right leg over your left leg and touch your right knee to the floor. Roll to the right and touch your left knee to the floor. Continue this knee-touch-roll back and forth for several bars.

C. Again on your left hip, kick your right leg out and over your left leg. Repeat on your right hip. Keep up the continuous rolling motion.

D. Catch the end of a left leg kick, place your left leg behind you by bending your knee. Swing onto your right hip, lean on your right hand. Roll your legs forward to the Basic Floor Roll position. Repeat on the other side. Rock back and forth as many times as you want.

E. Roll onto your right hip and bend both legs back to the left side. Reverse by stretching both legs forward and bending both knees back to the right side and roll onto your left hip.

The rhythm is: (A) roll right and left as you stretch and roll; (B) bend one knee and touch; (C) kick; (D) bend one knee; (E) bend both knees back.

Tummy Roll #1

A. Begin from the Basic Floor Roll position (top of page 102). Roll onto the top of your left thigh, bending your right knee.

B. Continue the roll until your tummy touches the floor. Supporting yourself on your hands, roll back up to the basic position and repeat the roll to the right side.

Tummy Roll #2

A. Begin with your knees bent, feet together and flat on the floor. Lean back on your arms.

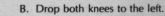

B. Drop both knees to the left.

C. Now roll over until your tummy touches the floor.

D. Let the momentum of the roll carry you until your feet touch the floor on your right side. Roll back to the beginning position. Do the same roll on the other side. Repeat the sequence in a winding and unwinding motion from side to side many times.

Rolling Kick-Up

A. Beginning from the Basic Floor Roll position (page 102), cross your right leg over your left leg and twist your torso to the left.

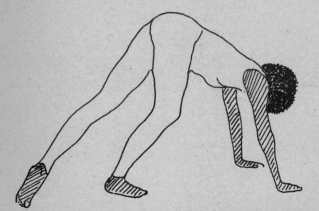

B. Lift your body so that your weight shifts to your hands and right leg.

C. Kick your left leg behind you as high as it will go. Drop your left leg to the floor as you let your body roll back into the basic position. Repeat the sequence with your other leg. Kick and roll, right and left at least eight times.

JAZZ FLOOR FUN   107

UP ON YOUR FEET

Now that you've completed your last floor fun movement, it's time to stand again. How do you do it without a struggle? Easily. And gracefully. Every movement is planned to flow from one into the other, and you'll learn how, using the different ascents in the following sequences.

Ascent #1

A. This ascent begins from the same basic rolling position that ends the floor roll routines. Roll to your right hip and bend your knees, feet behind you.

B. Swing up onto both knees and thrust your arms overhead, emphasizing the upward lift.

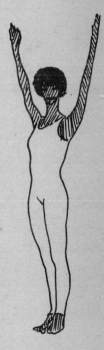

C. Place your left foot firmly on the floor as you begin to stand.

D. Place your right foot on the floor as you stand up, arms extended overhead. You are up on your feet in four easy movements, ready to continue dancing.

Ascent #2

You can begin this ascent after completing a sequence of movements like those shown in the Four Corners exercises, pages 74–79.

A. Relax on your tummy with your hands beneath your shoulders and your toes curled under.

B. Your toes should be in this position so you can easily walk back in a flat-footed stance.

C. Lift your body up, balancing on your hands and feet.

D. Walk backward with your hands.

E. Continue walking backward with your hands, moving closer to your feet.

F. Straighten up your torso, STRETCH, and SMILE!

Ascent #3

You can begin this from the Rolling Kick-Up, page 106.

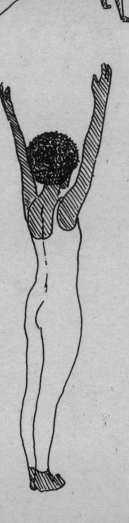

A. You are in this position, finishing the Rolling Kick-Up. Then . . .

B. . . . lower your leg and walk back with your hands as in Ascent #2 until you are standing straight with your arms overhead. Your back is to the audience— whether real or imaginary.

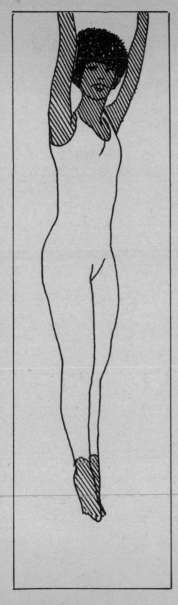

C. Jump around one-half turn, and you will be facing forward. Make the jump as high as you can, ending on a final, cheerful note. As your feet touch the floor, you'll be ready for a bow, smiling and feeling fantastic!

6 Dance the Inches Away

It's fun to see how high you can jump when you do the Flick-Kick. Jazz pants help give you a jazzy, jivy look.

To put extra punch in your jazzercise program, you can add an infinite variety of fancy foot patterns. They are joyful and bouncy. They will make you glimmer and glow, move and groove . . . and breathe heavily. It's all part of the total benefits. The rhythmic, springy, fast-paced dancing increases your need for oxygen, the essential ingredient of aerobic exercise philosophy. Your heart and lungs (cardiovascular system) work harder in a healthy way to improve your circulation, make you fit, and keep you that way. Put as much energy as you can into each Scoot, Flick-Kick, and Chasse, and you'll burn up calories. What could be a better bonus?

Be creative with the steps and patterns shown, and certainly try to develop more of your own. Listen to the music and fit the steps to it. Note how many times the basic melody repeats, and decide which dance steps you want to do to that melody. When the melody changes, change your step. Pace your dancing to the beat of the music. Terrific practice songs are Harvey Mason's "Marching in the Street" and Isaac Hayes's "Disco Connection."

JAZZ BATTEMENT (KICK)

All those marvelous floor stretches have loosened up your legs so that you can use them in high kick movements. For practice, try George Benson's "Breezin'" or a similar jazz selection.

Forward

A. Stand tall, arms relaxed at your sides. Place your left leg behind you, making sure your left heel touches the floor. Right leg is bent.

B. Swing your left knee up and straight forward. Return to position A.

C. Swing your left leg straight forward as high as possible in a sharp kick. Return to the first position. Repeat the Battement sequence with your right leg. The rhythm is: stretch, lift the knee, stretch, kick high.

To the Side

A. Cross your left leg behind your right leg and press your left heel to the floor. Arms are extended high and out.

B. Swing your left knee up and to the left side and return to position A.

C. Kick your left leg up high to the left side.

The rhythm is: cross, lift the knee, cross, kick high. Repeat with the other leg. Do the Jazz Battement at least eight times with each leg.

THE SCOOT

The Scoot is cute to see and cute to do. It's a staccatolike movement that emphasizes the downbeat of the music. Scooting provides a good transition between patterns of steps.

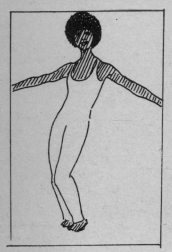

A. With your feet together, knees slightly bent, arms extended outward, do a small, sliding jump diagonally to your right.

B. Jump back to the center; your feet stay together.

C. Repeat the Scoot diagonally to the left. Continue the dance step in an alternating pattern: right, center, left, center.

118   JAZZERCISE

THE FLEA HOP

The Flea Hop combines easily with the Scoot for a peppy, jumpy routine that might be used with such songs as John Denver's "Thank God I'm a Country Boy" or the 1920s Charleston tune "Five Foot Two, Eyes of Blue."

A. Lift your right knee and hip to the right, hop to the right on your left foot.

B. Change position by stepping onto your right foot. Lift your left knee and hip to the left, hop to the left on your right foot.

The Flea Hop offers a rhythmic hop, step, hop, step from one foot to the other as it's done to the music.

THE FLICK-KICK

The Flick-Kick is a natural follow-through and/or combination with the Flea Hop and the Scoot. They are all jumping jazz movements designed to make a dance happy and zappy!

A. Lift your right foot behind you.

B. Flick and kick your right foot straight forward and hop lightly on your left foot.

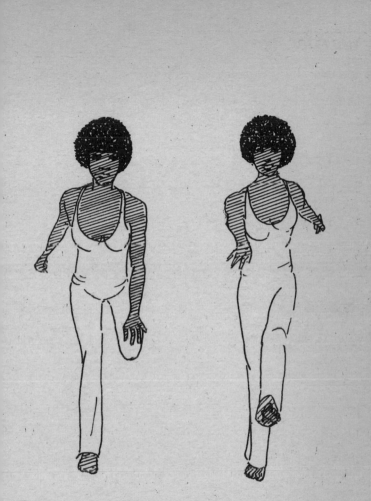

C. Jump onto your right foot and lift your left foot behind you.

D. Flick and kick your left foot straight forward and hop lightly on your right foot. Jump onto your left foot and return to the beginning position.

The rhythm is: flick-kick, jump, flick-kick, jump, alternating feet. It's a fun-to-do step that will take you from here to there and back again before you know what's happening!

THE STOMP

The Stomp is a jazz-rock movement. The feeling is heavier and earthier than the light, airy movements of the Flick-Kick and the Flea Hop. It has a definite downbeat, which you can emphasize by clapping. Select music recorded by The Average White Band, The Isley Brothers, or The Temptations.

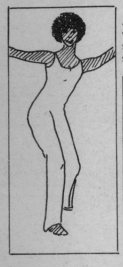

A. On the downbeat, stomp forward with your right foot, knees slightly bent and torso twisted somewhat left.

B. Bring your right foot together with the left and stand straight.

C. Again on the downbeat, stomp forward with your left foot, making sure it hits the floor flatly. Bring your left foot together with the right and stand straight. Repeat.

The beat is: stomp right, together, stomp left, together.

THE PUSH

This too is a jazz-rock step, a variation of the Stomp, which emphasizes the downbeat. Combine them in any way you want for a funky jazz pattern.

A. Touch your right toe and push your right hand diagonally to the right in a parallel line with your leg. Clap as you bring your feet together.

B. Repeat on the left side.

HEEL-TOE SHIFT

The Heel-Toe Shift combines the jazz-rock earthiness with the springy feeling of the Flick-Kick and the Flea Hop. Try it to the tune of Carly Simon and James Taylor's "Mockingbird." Follow the photos down, around, and up. The rhythm is: heel, toe, hop, shift, shift.

A. Touch your right heel out to the right side.

B. Turn your right toe in and touch it to the floor.

C. Lightly hop onto your right foot and . . .

D. . . . jump up, shift your body weight so you land on . . .

E. . . . your left foot with your right foot up.

F. Jump again and change feet.

G. Land on your right foot, with the left up, ready to begin again with the other foot.

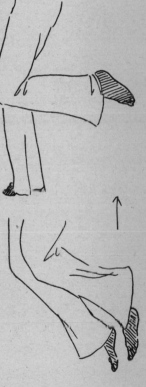

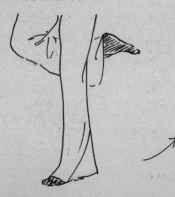

THE CHASSÉ (FOOT CHASE)

A light and airy side-to-side movement that adds variety to a dance routine by its directional change.

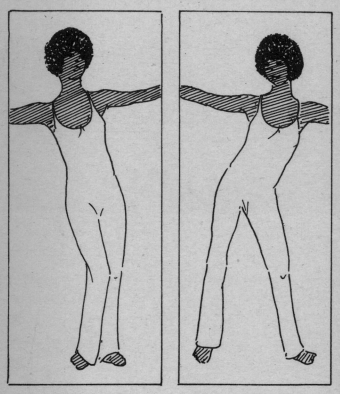

A. Feet together, right knee bent; you are poised, ready to step out.

B. Step out to the right with your right foot, isolating your right hip slightly.

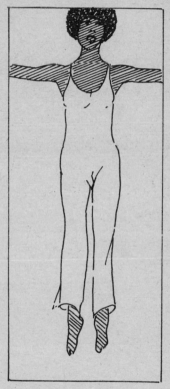 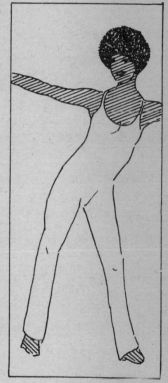

C. Push off of your right foot and jump straight up.

D. Land on your left foot, followed by your right foot. Repeat to the other side.

In this rhythm, the left foot is "chasing" the right. The step is: step out to the right, chase with the left, jump, land right. Step out to the left, chase with the right, jump, land left.

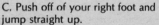

DANCE THE INCHES AWAY   127

THREE-STEP HIP LIFT

Now use the Hip Isolations you learned in Chapter 3, when you were "Limbering and Loosening," to their best advantage. The Three-Step Hip Lift is a side-to-side movement used for directional changes when dancing, and it combines easily with the Stomp. The rhythm is: step out and lift the hip, feet together, step out and dip. Do it first to the right side and then to the left side, alternating at least eight times.

Read across the pages ———➤

A. Step out to the right side and isolate your right hip, accenting it strongly as you lift it upward and to the side.

B. Close your left foot to your right food and . . .

C. . . . step your right foot to the right side, dipping to accent the downbeat, dramatizing the sideways motion.

D. To move to the left, step out with your left foot and isolate your left hip up and to the side. Again accent your hip movement.

E. Close your right foot to the left and . . .

F. . . . dip dramatically, moving your left foot to the left side.

128   JAZZERCISE

JAZZ SQUARE

The Jazz Square is a fundamental pattern that can be used as a transition between any of the preceding dance steps described, or between any others you may improvise. It enables you to shift your weight so you are in the proper position for the next step selected. The rhythm is: cross, back, side, forward.

A. Cross your right foot in front of and over your left foot.

B. Step back on your left foot and shift your weight from the front to the back, isolating your left hip back slightly.

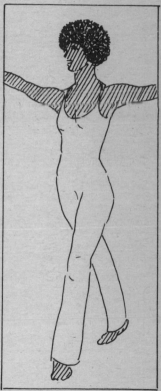

C. Step out to the right side, isolating your right hip slightly to the right.

D. Step forward on your left foot so your body is centered over your left leg in a firm and positive position.

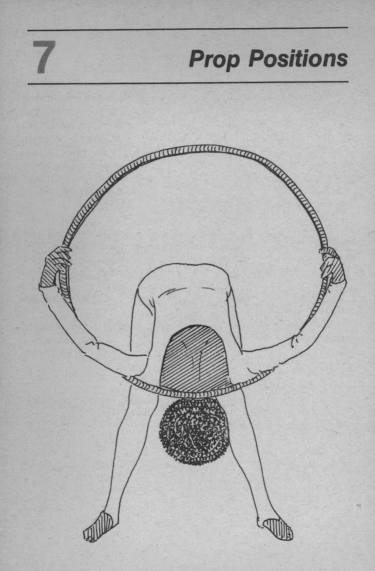

Many kinds of props may be used to add zest and interest to a routine. They vary the exercise fun too. Working with a hula hoop helps improve posture, keeping your shoulders and spine where they belong.

Ready for something more that you'll adore? The following "Prop" exercises and dance movements will add variety and excitement to every routine and give you more to work with than just your body. Balls, ropes, hoops, and wands increase your stretch-ability, give you an added feel for body placement, and a sense of coordination. Scandinavians pioneered the application of props with which to exercise; now gymnasts and dancers frequently use them for special effects and to create spectacular routines.

Props are fun to work with; they offer novel, unconventional movements with specific purposes. The ball jazzercises establish balance and increase eye-hand coordination. The rope is used for more than jumping; it stretches many parts of your body farther than you could ever stretch them without it. The hoop and wand exercises improve posture and body alignment so you will stand straight and tall. They trim the waistline too.

The jazz barré, the same kind of barré that ballet dancers use, is perfect for jazz stretching. The series of barré exercises will enable you to balance better as you stretch and pull with concentrated effort.

"ON THE BALL"

The best size ball is about twelve inches in diameter—the size
and feel of a volleyball. It should be sturdy so it won't squash,
squeeze, or break during the exercises. Try this to lilting music
such as John Sebastian's "What a Day for a Daydream," "Did
You Ever Have to Make up Your Mind," or "Warm Baby."

Roller #1

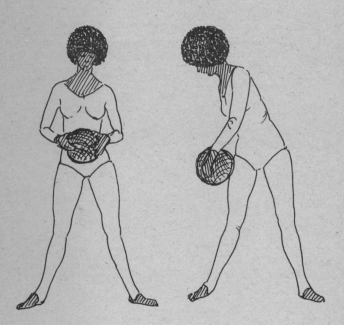

A. Stand with your feet apart and
hold the ball in front of your
stomach with both hands.

B. Roll the ball over and onto
your right thigh, keeping your
feet flat on the floor.

C. Continue rolling the ball down the outside of your right leg . . .

D. . . . and onto the floor, stretching, stretching as far as you can go with your feet flat on the floor.

Roll the ball back to your right foot, up along your leg to your right thigh, then onto your tummy. Repeat Roller #1 to the left and then follow through with Roller #2.

Roller #2

A. Begin from the last position to the left in Roller #1. Bend from your hips with your back flat, knees straight, legs apart. Push the ball so it rolls along the floor to the right side. Catch it with your right hand.

B. Push the ball back so it rolls back along the floor to the left side. Open your arms for a good stretch.

C. Catch the ball with your left hand. Stretch as far as you can, bending your left knee in a lunge. Roll the ball back and forth to the rhythm of the music.

The Dip

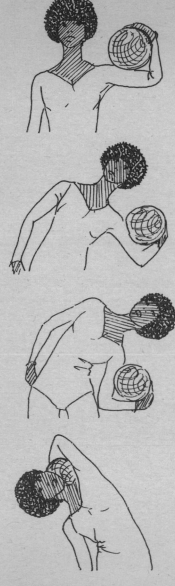

A. Place the ball on top of your left shoulder and hold it with your left hand. Squeeze the ball tightly. This will tighten the underarm.

B. Begin to dip to your left side.

C. Continue to dip until your elbow touches your left hip.

D. Lift the ball and roll it behind your neck for a bonus waistline stretch. Repeat A to D to the right.

The Squeezes

HIP SWING

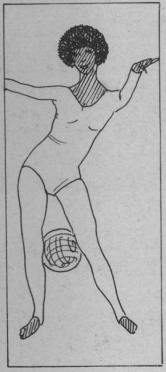

A. Put the ball between your knees and squeeze the ball tightly.

B. With a swinging motion, isolate your hip to the right and then to the left without dropping the ball. This is a terrific exercise for the inside thigh when it is done back and forth many times.

TWIST JUMP

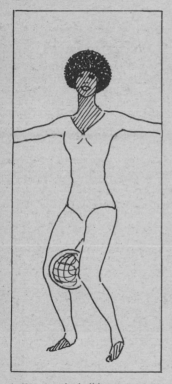 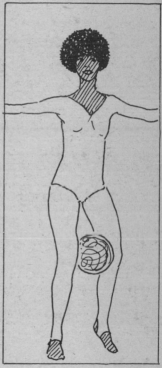

A. Keeping the ball between your knees, follow the movement through from the Hip Swing to the Twist Jump. Twist your body and jump to the right . . .

B. . . . and to the left. Repeat several times. Alternate the Hip Swing and the Twist Jump for great fun and agility. And Smile!

On Top

Continue to work with the ball for these exercises which are designed to help you find your center of gravity and improve your balance. They'll result in slimmer legs and tighter tummies too.

#1

A. Perch on the ball with your knees bent, feet together flat on the floor, your arms behind you, supporting your upper body weight.

Read across the pages ⟶

#2

A. With your feet planted firmly on the floor, balance as you sit on top of the ball. Cross your arms at your chest.

B. Sharply, in almost a jumping motion, extend your left leg out to the side in Russian Cossack dance fashion. Return your left leg to the beginning position and repeat with your right leg. Alternate legs, feeling the balance and the rhythm of the movement.

JAZZERCISE

B. When you feel you are balanced sufficiently, kick your left leg up quickly, sharply. Return your foot to the floor and kick up with the other leg. Alternate the legs many times until you get the feel of balancing while you are perched on top of the ball.

C. When you feel you're ready, kick up both legs quickly. Balance for a second or two and return your feet to the floor. Repeat several times.

C. Now add the arm movements. Bring your elbows into your sides and tighten.

D. Thrust your arms overhead each time you kick each leg, and then into your sides each time you bring your feet together. The rhythm is: together, out, together, out—in time with the music.

KNOWING THE ROPES

Select a length of sturdy, non-stretchy cord, such as clothesline or jute, about three yards long, or long enough for a jump rope. You may use it for jumping, but for the following stretch movements, fold it in half and tie a knot on each end. Pack the rope when you travel; it will make it easier to exercise when you are away from home and unable to attend a class. For music, use Lou Rawls's "Natural Man" or David Nichtern's "Midnight at the Oasis" sung by Maria Muldaur.

Twist Lunge

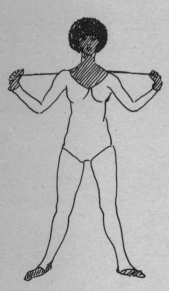

A. Fold the rope in half and hold it stretched behind your neck as shown. Keep the rope taut.

B. Twist your body to the left and lunge to the left, bending your left knee. Return to center, twist, and lunge to the right. Back and forth, back and forth to a musical rhythm until you can feel your midriff pull, stretch, and tighten.

JAZZERCISE

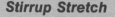

Stirrup Stretch

A. Sit on the floor, stretch your legs forward, and lock your knees. Place the rope under your left foot. Hold the rope short if you're very flexible, longer if you're just beginning these stretches. With practice, you'll discover you can hold the rope shorter and shorter—positive proof that you are becoming more and more flexible.

B. Lift your chest and bend your left knee.

C. Stretch your leg as high as possible, pulling it up with the rope.

D. Swing your leg to the side and stretch higher. Return your leg to the floor. Repeat the same stretch sequence with your right leg. Alternate legs until you feel loose and supple.

Seated Rope Jump

A. Sit on the floor with your legs outstretched. Hold the rope slack behind your neck.

B. As you lift your legs and bend your knees to your chest, swing the rope around your feet and under your legs.

C. Pull the rope until it touches the back of your thighs. Thrust your legs slightly forward as you balance on your derrière. Bring the rope from under your legs and up to the back of your neck as you return your legs to the floor. Try using one leg at a time too.

Stretch Away

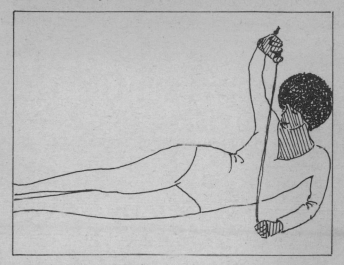

A. Stretch out on your left side and support your weight on your elbow. Hold the rope taut, perpendicular to the floor, in front of your chest.

B. As you swing your right leg to the back, your right arm swings forward. The result is a long, long stretch for your waistline and outer thigh.

HOOP-LA

An easy-to-use prop is a child's hula hoop, available in toy departments. Their gay, bright colors add a happy note to exercising. In dance routines, the hoops are sometimes painted with fluorescent colors and used under black lights. A stunning routine is worked out for you on page 177 (Chapter 8, Routine #10).

The Drop

Read across the pages ⟶

A. Stand tall, feet together. Hold the hoop from the inside, high overhead.

B. Drop the hoop to your shoulders.

C. Bend your knees and drop the hoop until it touches the floor. Lift the hoop up again and overhead. Repeat up and down, up and down. Follow through with the next movement on page 148.

Standing Pick-Up

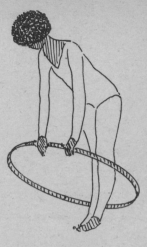

A. Stand in the center of the hoop with your knees locked; bend over forward and grasp the hoop from the outside.

B. Begin to lift the front of the hoop.

C. Stand straight and touch the front of the hoop to your thighs. Bend over, returning the hoop to the floor as in position A. Bend over and up, over and up.

The Tip

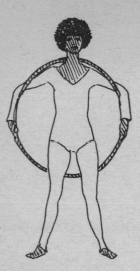

A. Stand straight, feet apart. Place the hoop so that it rests on the back of your neck. Wrap your arms around the outside of the hoop.

B. Tip the hoop to the left as you bend to the side from your waist.

C. Leaning to the left side, lift your right leg until it is parallel to the floor. Return to position A. Repeat to the right side. Continue the movement, left to right, until its momentum carries you easily from side to side, balancing securely as you "tip."

The Lunge

A. Stand with your feet apart. Rest the hoop on the small of your back and hold it from the outside.

B. Lean slightly back and to the left. Bending your left knee, isolate your right hip to the right.

C. Lunge over to the right and swing the hoop over your head and forward to a waist-high level.

D. Emphasize the lunge as you lean forward until the hoop touches the floor. Lift back up to center. Bend and lunge to the other side. Repeat: lunge to right, return to center, lunge to left, return to center, and so forth.

Seated Pick-Up

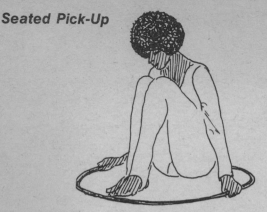

A. Sit within the hoop with your knees bent. Grasp the outside of the hoop.

B. With a quick shooting motion, stretch the hoop overhead and your legs straight forward on the floor. Return to position A and repeat the entire motion: bend in, shoot out, bend in, shoot out. This will tone and stretch the muscles in your lower abdomen.

Roll About

A. Stretch your legs wide apart. Place the rim of the hoop on the floor in front of you.

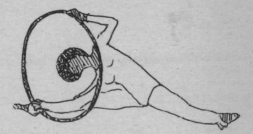

B. Roll the hoop on the floor toward your right toe and stretch as far as you can.

C. Roll it back to center and then to the left. Roll it back and forth, right to left, until you feel a good stretch in your waist and hips. This will give your thighs a slim and sleek body line.

MAGIC WAND

There's no sleight of hand when you do the following exercises, even though you will feel extra inches melting away magically. Using a long wandlike stick as an exercise and dance aid is novel—and EXTREMELY beneficial. You'll become more aware of your muscles and how they move in relation to one another. It's a posture "prop-er upper" too. For your magic wand, use a broom handle or a sturdy dowel, three quarters to an inch thick, available at a lumberyard. It should be long enough to reach up to chest level. Be sure your wand is sanded smooth so you don't get splinters in your hands.

Bouncing

A. Place one end of the wand on the floor, holding onto the top of the other end. Bend from your hips and stretch forward. Keep your arms as straight as possible, your feet together and flat on the floor, knees locked. Bounce your upper torso up and down, up and down, stretching farther and farther out with each bounce. Follow the Bouncing with the Walking Stick.

Walking Stick

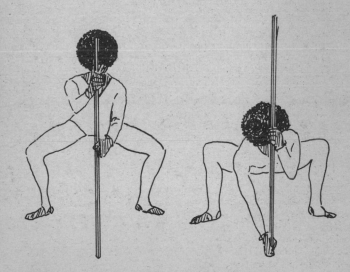

A. In the same position as in Bouncing, stand with your feet apart, holding the wand in front of you at arms' length.

B. "Walk" your hands down the wand, bending your knees as your hands alternate their grip on their downward walk.

C. "Walk" your hands all the way to the floor, touch, and hold. Walk your hands back up to the top of the wand. Repeat walking: up, down, up, stretching and bending your knees, resulting in a magical toning of your thighs.

Shoulder Drop

You'll be conjuring obvious benefits to your waistline as you drop your shoulders from side to side, holding on to the magic wand.

A. Place the wand behind your neck, grasping it from the back near the ends. Your feet are apart, flat on the floor.

B. Drop your right shoulder and bend from your waist. Return to center and drop your left shoulder to the left. Return to center. Repeat the drop right and left as often as you like.

Elbow-Shoulder Drop

A. In the same position as in the Shoulder Drop, hook your elbows over the top of the wand.

B. Drop your left shoulder to the left, bending from your waist. Return to center and drop your right shoulder to the right. You can see how beautifully this exercise flexes your back muscles and helps improve your posture as you drop right and left, right and left.

Back Stretch

Your magic wand can strengthen and beautify the body line along your back.

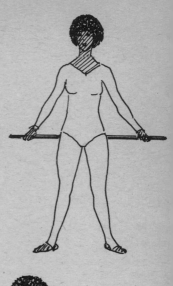

A. Place your feet apart and hold the wand behind you at hip level.

B. Stretch your rib cage forward and lift the wand back and up, keeping your arms straight. Feel your rib cage lift up out of your waistline with each lift of the wand. Return the wand to hip level, relaxing your rib cage and back muscles. Do this to a percussive rhythm. Repeat as often as you like.

Sorcerer's Swing

It's time to get some swing into your sorcery. Twisting will work wonders for your waist.

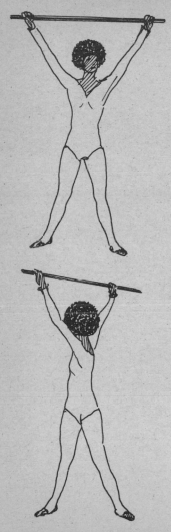

A. Hold the wand at each end with your arms stretched high overhead.

B. Swing and twist your torso to the right. Continue the swing through center and then to the left.

JAZZ BARRÉ

Since you probably don't have a jazz dance barré in your home, hold onto the edge of your kitchen sink or a piece of heavy furniture. You may also mount a towel bar on a wall at about waist level. Make sure you have room to swing in and out, back and forth, and side to side. Use songs in Lee Oskar's album to accompany your Jazz Barré movements.

Barré Fly

A. Feet together, stand away from the barré at elbow's length. Hold the barré with your left hand. Touch your hips onto the barré, knees locked. Dip your right shoulder down to the right with your elbow touching your hip.

B. Push your hips out to the right and stretch your right arm out and overhead so your body forms a graceful curve away from the barré. Repeat this swinging motion in and out several times to the right. Then turn around, hold the barré with your right hand, and repeat to the other side. Stretch, stretch from your waist until you feel the pull on each side.

Over-Upper

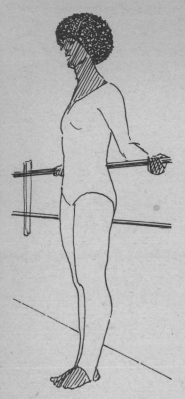

A. Stand with your feet together and your back against the barré. Hold onto it with both hands.

B. Bend over from your hips and stretch your chest down, back flat.

C. Drop over and try to touch your nose to your knees. Return to the "up" position and repeat: up, over, down.

Hips Ahoy

A Jazz Barré movement that swishes away inches from your middle, your hips, and your back. The rhythm is: stand tall, arch back, swing right, swing left.

A. Stand with your hips toward the barré; hold onto it with your hands far apart, feet together.

B. Arch your back, and drop your head backward.

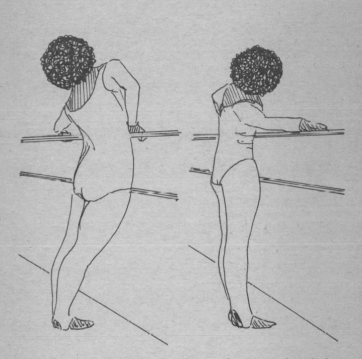

C. Straighten up and swing your hips to the right; keep your knees locked and your hands in place . . .

D. . . . then swing through the center and to your left. Repeat the sequence: back, up, right, left at least four times.

Not Just for Kicks

These simple exercises are for more than kicks; they're fun, but they turn problem areas, such as hips and thighs, into delightful smoothies.

#1

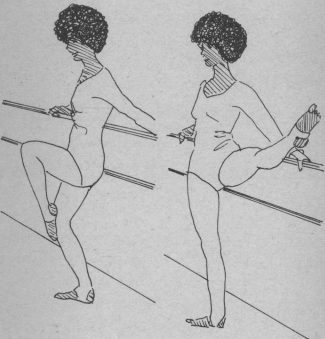

A. Stand with your back to the barré. Hold on with your hands far apart. Bend your left knee and touch your left toe to your right knee. Swing your left knee to the right, back to center, and . . .

B. . . . kick out to the left. Bend your leg to the toe-touch-knee position again, swing to the right, and kick out to the left. The rhythm is: bend, swing right, kick out left. Repeat several times using each leg.

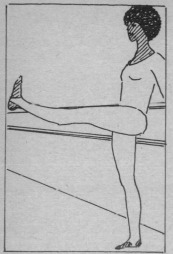

#2

Back against the barre, hold on with your hands far apart. With the foot flexed, kick your left leg up to waist level in front of you and hold. Repeat with each leg several times.

#3

With your left side to the barré, hold on with your left hand and place your right hand on your right hip. Kick your right leg, foot flexed, to the right side. Always keep the knee pointing forward (an excellent position for working on outside thigh excess). Repeat this kick several times with each leg.

In the preceding chapters, you learned a variety of steps and movements that can be combined to form basic jazzercise dance. Each has been introduced to you gradually to prepare you for dance routines. Now that you are familiar with the terms, you should be able to move easily from an Isolation to a Leg Fly-Away to a Jazz Square.

The ten routines that follow have been developed as dance movements set to the flow of selected music; that is, they have been choreographed. "Choreography," the art of creating and arranging steps, moves, stretches, and transitions to fit specific music for specific purposes, can make jazzercise dance unique. Each routine is designed to fit a specific song and to improve the body with total fitness as the goal.

Chuck Mangione's "Chase the Clouds Away" (Routine #1) is a flowing, lyrical tune that suggests easy, gliding, stretchy movements which are perfect for loosening and limbering. For contrast, Leo Sayer's "Long Tall Glasses" (Routine #3), an up-tempo song with a strong, fast beat, is choreographed with snappy, energetic movements that put your heart and lungs in healthy action.

Ideally, you should learn all ten routines and schedule them into a tri-weekly, bi-weekly, or, best of all, a daily program. Build on the ideas of these choreographed sequences by applying them to other songs, using your own interpretations and creative improvisations.

ROUTINES

Note: R = right
L = left
Cts. = counts of the music for each movement

Routine #1

You are ready for this first routine when you have practiced the movements through page 43. Use it for warming up.

Music: "Chase the Clouds Away"—Chuck Mangione

Introduction:
Stretch overhead with both hands
Round over and drop to the floor. Spine Tinglers   p. 40
beginning position. Repeat one Spine Tinglers
sequence to the end of the musical introduction
THINK STRE-E-E-TCHY!

Part 1: Follow the medium tempo pace of the music
Take 2 cts. for each movement
8 Readys of the Warm-Up   p. 18–19
Open feet—4 cts. for each movement
6 Sets of the Warm-Up   p. 20–21
Take 2 cts. for each movement

Part 2:
8 Jazz Pliés in First Position   p. 42
Take 2 cts. for each movement
8 Jazz Pliés in Second Position   p. 43
Take 2 cts. for each movement

Part 3:
Repeat Part 2 without opening feet
End the routine with the Go sequence of the
Warm-Up   p. 21
Take 2 cts. for each movement
Repeat as many times as needed to the end of the
record

Routine #2

This routine concentrates on your top torso and waistline, using movements through page 59 in graceful, flowing, lyrical sequences.

Music: "Cast Your Fate to the Wind"—Quincy Jones

Introduction:
    2 Jazz Hands sequences   p. 30
        Take 2 cts. for each sequence
    4 Finger Squeeze sequences on each hand   p. 31
        Take 1 ct. for each movement
Be precise as well as graceful and flowing.

Part 1:
    4 Elbow Thrust Stretches with the R arm   p. 48
        Take 4 cts. for each
    4 Elbow Thrust Stretches with the L arm
        Take 4 cts. for each
    8 Elbow Thrust Stretches with both arms
        Take 4 cts. for each
  10 Elbow Thrust Stretches with both arms,
     ending with the stretch overhead instead of
     to the side
        Take 4 cts. for each

Part 2:
    4 Single Triangles with the R arm   p. 50
        Take 2 cts. for each
    4 Single Triangles with the L arm
        Take 2 cts. for each
    4 Double Triangles on R side   p. 51
        Take 2 cts. for each
    4 Double Triangles on L side
        Take 2 cts. for each
Repeat Double Triangle R and L side as above

Part 3:
    8 Elbow Squares. Use only the up-and-down   p. 49
     sequence
        Take 2 cts. for each
    8 Elbow Squares, using the side-to-side sequence
        Take 2 cts. for each
Repeat Part 3 two more times

Routine #3

A super-fun routine that will increase your cardiovascular rate, firm and thin your thighs.

Music: "Long Tall Glasses"—Leo Sayer

Routine #4

If your shoulders and back are tired from sitting all day or standing in one place too long, this will feel good and help get you moving again.

Music: "Willie and the Hand Jive"—Eric Clapton

Introduction:
    Stand with your feet apart in Second Position.   p. 44
    Your hands alongside your body. Bounce
    to the beat of the music while opening and
    closing your hands.

Part 1:
    8 Hand Jives—sequence A   p. 54
        Take 2 cts. for each
    8 Hand Jives—sequence B   p. 54
        Take 2 cts. for each
    8 Hand Jives—sequence C   p. 54
        Take 2 cts. for each
    8 Hand Jives—sequence D   p. 54
        Take 2 cts. for each
    Repeat Part 1

Part 2:
    10 Wings and   ⎫ Combine the Wing arm move-   p. 53
    Crazy Pliés #2 ⎬ ments with the Crazy Pliés   p. 64
        Take 2 cts. for each
    16 Pushes, alternating R and L feet   p. 123
        Take 2 cts. for each
    Repeat Part 2

Part 3:
    Repeat sequence A and B of Part 1 to end of song.
    Finish in a pose with arms stretched overhead
    and hands in an open Jazz Hands position. Feet
    together. SMILE.

Routine #5

Your tummy and midriff will welcome this toning and tightening to music. Try parts of it any time of the day when the music and movements come to mind.

Music: "Fever"—Peggy Lee

Introduction:
 Feet together. 8 Forward-Back Rib Cage   p. 32
 Isolations to the beat of the music.
  Take 4 cts. for each

Part 1:
 Continue to isolate rib cage then stretch your arms
  out to the side.
 8 Forward-Back Rib Cage Isolations
  Take 4 cts. for each set
 8 Side-to-Side Rib Cage Isolations   p. 32
  Take 2 cts. for each set
 Repeat Part 1

Part 2:
 8 Rib Cage Squares. Begin rotation to R p. 33
  Take 8 cts. for each square
 8 Rib Cage Squares, rotating to L
  Take 8 cts. for each square

Part 3:
 8 Jazz Struts, alternating R and L   p. 60
  Take 4 cts. for each strut
 8 Jazz Leans, alternating R and L   p. 61
  Take 4 cts. for each lean
 Repeat Part 3

Part 4:
 1 Descent #2 to the floor   p. 71
  Take 4 cts. for each position in the descent
 You are now in a Jazz Split position. Stay in this
 position for your next routine. Routine #5
 emphasizes slow stretching movements and will
 prepare you for the floor movements in the next
 routine.

Routine #6

This marvelous leg stretch routine will make you feel marvelous all over while stretching out all the "kinks!"

Music: "Exactly Like You"—Morris Stoloff Orchestra

Introduction:
Beginning in the Jazz Split position (from the ending of Routine #5), bounce your chest forward over your right leg in time to the music.

Part 1:
2 Jazz Split sequences   p. 92–93
   Take 2 cts. for each movement of the sequence
   Move forward stretched leg into the Indian Cross position   p. 80

Part 2:
8 Indian Cross B lifts   p. 80
   Take 2 cts. for each lift
4 Indian Cross C stretches in a bounce stretch   p. 80
motion
   Take 2 cts. for each position
Repeat Parts 1 and 2
Transition: Bend both knees quickly into your chest and move your legs into a left Jazz Split and swing into . . . or . . .
Repeat Parts 1 and 2 on the L side
Transition: Bend both knees into your chest, taking 4 cts. Stretch both legs forward in the Long Sit (page 96). Bounce chest over legs until the end of the song. As you bounce, STRE-E-E-TCH as far forward as you can. Think LO-O-ONG . . . THI-I-I-N . . . Thoughts

Routine #7

Another good tummy tightener and toner that ties right in with the earlier routines. It's fun to "swing" right through this one!

Music: "Workin' at the Car Wash Blues"—Jim Croce

Introduction:
Stretch over the Long Sit position, A, and bounce   p. 96
your chest forward to the beat of the music until
the end of the introduction.

Part 1:
8 Swing Unders   p. 96
    Take 4 cts. for each movement
8 Long Sit-Up Swings   p. 97
    Take 2 cts. for each movement

Part 2:
8 Sit-Up Swings   p. 97
    Take 2 cts. for each movement
8 Swing Unders   p. 96
    Take 4 cts. for each movement

Part 3:
8 Swinging Shoulder Stands   p. 98–99
    Take 4 cts. to roll up to shoulders
    and 4 cts. to roll down
8 Swing Unders   p. 96
    Take 4 cts. for each Swing Under
8 Swinging Shoulder Stands to end of music
End in Long Sit position with arms stretched
overhead

Routine #8

This routine will "thump" and "bump" inches from your hips plus flatten your abdomen and slim your waist. A "3-in-1" routine!

Music: "Sunshine Keri"—Lee Oskar

Introduction:
Begin in Basic Floor Roll position A. Bounce back   p. 102
of knees on floor in time to the music until the
end of the introduction.

Part 1:
16 Bumper Thumpers, position A, alternating   p. 102
    R and L
     Take 2 cts. for each
16 Bumper Thumpers, position C, alternating   p. 103
    R and L
     Take 8 cts. for each

Part 2:
On the last Bumper Thumper, position C, hold
the L leg in a stretched position and cross it over
the right, settling into the Cross-Over Lift position   p. 90–91
8 Cross-Over Lifts, sequence A to D, L side
    Take 8 cts. for each
8 Cross-Over Lifts, sequence A to D, R side
    Take 8 cts. for each

Part 3:
20 Rolling Kick-Ups, alternating R and L. Pause   p. 106–7
   slightly for 2 cts. as the leg extends in the air
     Take 8 cts. for each
On the last Rolling Kick-Up, hold your leg high
for 2 cts. Bring that leg down to meet the other and
do the Up on Your Feet Ascent #3. You are now   p. 112
standing again.
Jump up and swing around. You're doing great!

Routine *#9*

When you near the end of your "program," you'll want to cool down, and this dance will do it. Take it nice and easy, letting the movement flow.

Music: "There's a Kind of Hush"—Carpenters

Introduction:
The Scoot. Repeat, alternating R and L for the   p. 118
duration of the introduction.
    Take 2 cts. for each Scoot

Part 1:
4 Jazz Battlement Forward sequences using the R   p. 116
leg
        Take 2 cts. for each movement of the
            sequence
4 Jazz Battement Forward sequences with the L
leg
        Take 2 cts. for each movement of the
            sequence

Part 2:
8 Jazz Squares, beginning with the R foot   p. 130-1
        Take 1 ct. for each movement in the
            sequence
8 Three-Step Hip Lifts; alternate R and L   p. 128-9
        Take 4 cts. for each movement in the
            sequence
8 Jazz Squares as above

Part 3:
2 R Leg Fly-Aways, A to D only   p. 66
        Take 2 cts. for each sequence
2 L Leg Fly-Aways, A to D only
        Take 2 cts. for each sequence
Finish in the poised stance, and you're FEELING
KIND OF FINE!

Routine #10

The Prop Positions can suggest many routines. Here is one with the hoop.

Music: "Swingin' Shepherd Blues"—Moe Koffman Quartet

Introduction:
  12 Hoop Drops   p. 146–7
    Take 4 cts. for each
  Transition: On the last "drop" to the floor, leave the hoop there and stand up with your hands overhead. With the next note of the song, bend over and begin . . .
  12 Standing Pick-Ups   p. 148
    Take 4 cts. for each
  Transition: On the last "lift" of the hoop, return it quickly to the floor and sit inside it. Go on to . . .

Part 2:
  12 Seated Pick-Ups   p. 152
    Take 4 cts. for each
  Transition: On the last "lift," open your legs wide and continue the movement into . . .
  8 Roll Abouts   p. 153
    Take 4 cts. for each
  Transition: On the last Roll About to the left, pick up the hoop and thrust it over your head. Continue with . . .
  4 Seated Pick-Ups   p. 152
    Take 4 cts. for each
  Transition: On the fourth Seated Pick-Up, stand up as you thrust the hoop overhead. Then drop the rim of the hoop to the small of your back.

Part 3:
  4 Lunges R, 4 Lunges L, repeat 4 Lunges to R   p. 150–1
    Take 4 cts. for each
  Transition: Stretch quickly and bring the hoop overhead. After the last Lunge to the R, end the routine with a deep bow (page 132). You LOOK GORGEOUS from every angle.

Sometimes the simpler the costume, the more dramatic. Sequined arrows and arm bands are used with leotards and jazz pants. The arrows can be removed if they are applied with Velcro or are basted on.
Photo: Jay Wexler

When you feel good about yourself, and you like the way you look, you may want the whole world to know. Your happiness and joy can affect others in a positive way. Many new students are attracted to jazz classes as a result of seeing other students perform, not necessarily as professionals, but as enlightened amateurs.

There are many opportunities for the amateur dancer working with a small dance group, especially a group attuned to the benefits of body conditioning. A dance performance can be spiced up with a short lecture-demonstration on its health aspects as well as the fun and joy of learning the jazzercise method as an alternative to ordinary exercise.

Service clubs always seek interesting programs that reflect the contemparary scene. Amateur groups often are invited to perform at shopping centers. Such performances attract customers and provide excellent exposure for your group. Countless groups and individuals have landed parts in local community theater musicals in this way. It can provide a marvelous opening into a new field of activity; at the same time, you'll gain confidence in yourself and in your ability to perform. You'll meet new people with a wide range of interests that will make you and your life more fascinating.

When you decide to participate in a public performance, there are several suggestions that will make you, your audience, and your client anxious for a return engagement.

Costuming

It takes little jazz to create a costume with pizzazz. Effective costuming can be accomplished by using basic leotards and tights. To add extra swing to any movement, wrap a flared skirt around a leotard or add a bit of fringe around the waist or neckline. Trim a leotard with a sequined belt, a choker, or bright-colored scarf.

Where stage lighting will accompany a performance, you might want to think about using different fabric textures. Lighting plays beautifully on iridescent satins, glittering sequins, and beads.

You can get ideas for costumes by watching dancers on television and in stage performances, or by thumbing through *Dance* magazine, an excellent trade publication for dancers. Your library will often have a picture file that you can consult as well as many books on musical films of the twenties and thirties. Use your own creativity and imagination and have a good time doing it! The costumes worn by dancers in the photos will provide additional ideas.

Technical Aspects

Whenever possible, take a close look at the area where you will be dancing. It's important to know its dimensions so that you can adjust your routines to the space available. Note the surface of the performing area as well. Often, it can be slippery or difficult to dance on. If you are not on an elevated platform, be sure to do mostly standing routines. ·

You will usually need to bring your own sound equipment (either a tape recorder or record player with additional speakers). If you are doing a lecture-demonstration, you may also require a microphone. Pretest the sound system. Many good programs and demonstrations are spoiled because the music is too soft or too loud. This can be distracting and irritating to an audience.

Make sure the lighting is adequate and that electrical outlets are nearby and plentiful (for the sound equipment). Always take extra extension cords.

All financial arrangements should be clearly understood before you accept an engagement. Many of the performances will be done gratis. Occasionally, you may be given a token donation to help you defray the expenses of travel, music, or costuming. You may want to establish a policy with your group, deciding how any extra money should be used.

Attitude

Always be on time.

Plan a diversified dance program that will appeal to everyone. Include slow routines as well as the "jumpiest jazz" and the "resoundingest rock" in your repertoire. Always think positively and, when performing, radiate a feeling of happiness about what you have to offer. Your audience will turn on to jazzercise as it watches you perform the unique movements

An easy-to-make, wraparound skirt used over leotards and tights gives a flowing effect. The skirt can match or contrast. Left: Anna Wolf. Right: Nikki Miller.

with a smile on your face and a spring in your step! These kinds of performances and lecture-demonstrations can inspire others to try dancing and moving in ways they never thought possible.

Remember that your enthusiasm can be contagious! It can spread like wildfire and give everyone you meet the chance to enjoy the well-being caused by JAZZERCISE!

Kathy Zanardelli wears a tie-dyed leotard with a sequined neck choker.

Kathy Malkmus wears a fringed satin top. The fringe bounces when the dancer bounces, and the satin catches the light. It's easy to make; select a blouse pattern with back snaps, and decorate it with fringe.

Satin shorts with white satin sashes, bow ties, and cuffs
over a basic leotard-tight combination give a thirties appearance
for a performance to the song "42nd Street." Front to back:
Jane Blackford, Anna Wolf, Kathy Acri, and Karen Linden.

Sashes can be tied around the neck or head for another quick costume change. They add a swing and shout a "with it" attitude. Front to back: Anne Burks, Kathy Malkmus, Kathy Zanardelli.

Anne Burks displays the happy attitude of the jazz dancer as she twirls a belt—another quick-change costume idea.

Cliff Smith does a Jazz Battement. He wears a stretch fabric jumpsuit that can be embellished using some of the same costume-change ideas shown for women.

Juan Ugarte performs a Split Jump in an outdoor rehearsal.

A well-rehearsed group dances precisely,
synchronizing movements to the music perfectly.

Music Recommendations

Selections are listed by chapters so that you may match music to the appropriate movements. Experiment and have fun!

Chapter 3

Temptations: Papa Was a Rollin' Stone (LP); Grover Washington: "Black Frost," Mister Magic (LP); Dr. Buzzard's Original Savannah Band: "Sour and Sweet;" Walter Murphy: "Rhapsody in Blue," "A Fifth of Beethoven;" Boz Skaggs: "Lowdown," "What Can I Say;" War: "L.A. Sunshine," "Heartbeat;" Deodato: *Very Together* (LP).

Chapter 4

Eric Clapton: "Willy and the Hand Jive;" Jazz Crusaders: "Put It Where You Want It;" John Denver: "Sunshine on My Shoulder," "Thank God I'm a Country Boy;" Janis Ian: "At Seventeen;" Scott Joplin: *The Red Back Book* (LP)—"The Cascades;" Loggins & Messina: "Your Mama Don't Dance;" Ringo Starr: "Occapella;" Tim Weisberg: "Listen to the City;" Natalie Cole: "I've Got Love On My Mind," "This Will be;" Spinners: "Rubberband Man," "You're Throwing a Good Love Away;" Elvis Presley: "Return to Sender;" Captain and Tennille: "Muskrat Love;" Glenn Campbell: "Sunflower;" Perry Botkin Jr.: "Nadia's Theme;" Manhattan Transfer: *"Scotch and Soda,"* "Java Jive," "Blue Champagne;" Pointer Sisters: "Going Down Slowly."

Chapter 5

Mark-Almond: "The City;" Jim Croce: "Bad, Bad Leroy Brown;" Bill Haley and the Comets: "(We're Gonna) Rock

Around the Clock," "Rock-A-Beatin' Boogie," "Shake, Rattle and Roll;" Rhythm Heritage: Theme from "S.W.A.T.;" Billy Preston: "I Wrote a Simple Song;" Neil Sedaka: "Nana's Song," "Breaking Up Is Hard to Do;" Stevie Wonder: "You Are the Sunshine of My Life," Songs in the Key of Life (LP); Dr. Buzzard's Original Savannah Band: "Cherchez La Femme;" Rose Royce: "Carwash;" Thelma Houston: "Today Will Soon Be Yesterday," "If It's the Last Thing I Do;" Natalie Cole: "Party Lights;" Elvis Presley: "Heartbreak Hotel," "Jailhouse Rock;" Jimmy Buffet: "Margaritaville."

Chapter 6

Grand Award Roaring 20's #2 (LP): "Five Foot Two, Eyes of Blue;" George Benson: "Breezin';" Isley Brothers: "Work to Do," "Fight the Power;" Isaac Hayes: "Disco Connection;" Harvey Mason: "Marching in the Street;" Carly Simon-James Taylor: "Mockingbird;" Average White Band: "Cut the Cake," "Pick up the Pieces;" K.C. and the Sunshine Band: "Wrap Your Arms Around Me," "Shake Your Bootie," "Boogie Shoes;" Maynard Ferguson: "Theme from Rocky;" Elvis Presley: "Blue Suede Shoes;" Wing and a Prayer Fife and Drum Corps: Baby Face (LP), Babyface Strikes Back (LP)— "Yes, We Have No Bananas," "Hernando's Hideaway;" Captain and Tennille: "Can't Stop Dancin';" Walter Murphy: "Flight 76;" Meco: Star Wars and Other Galactic Funk (LP); Leo Sayer: "How Much Love," "You Make Me Feel Like Dancing;" Stevie Wonder: "I Wish," "Sir Duke."

Chapter 7

David Nichtern: "Midnight at the Oasis;" Lee Oskar: "Sunshine Keri;" Lou Rawls: "Natural Man;" John Sebastian: "What a Day for a Daydream," "Did You Ever Have to Make Up Your Mind," "Warm Baby."

Ball   John Sebastian: "Welcome Back Kotter;" Melissa Manchester: "My Sweet Thing."

Rope   Les Paul and Chet Atkins: Lester and Chester (LP)— "It Had to Be You," "Birth of the Blues."

Hoop   Billy Preston: "Will It Go Round in Circles;" War: "Summer."

Wand   Ike and Tina Turner: "Proud Mary;" Rita Coolidge: "Higher and Higher."

Jazz Barré   Gap Mangione: *She* (LP).

Chapter 8

Carpenters: "There's a Kind of Hush;" Eric Clapton: "Willy and the Hand Jive;" Jim Croce: "Workin' at the Car Wash Blues;" Quincy Jones: "Cast Your Fate to the Wind;" Moe Koffman Quartet: "Swingin' Shepherd Blues;" Peggy Lee: "Fever;" Lee Oskar: "Sunshine Keri;" Chuck Mangione: "Chase the Clouds Away;" Leo Sayer: "Long Tall Glasses;" Morris Stoloff Orchestra: "Exactly Like You."

Supply Sources

*JAZZERCISE album with illustrated booklet. Coordinated with the ten routines in Chapter 8. Order from: Orion Records, 614 Davis Street, Evanston, Illinois 60201.

*JAZZERCISE cassette tapes with illustrated booklet. A variety of tapes consisting of ten assorted routines. Order from: Jazzercise, P.O. Box 1414, Vista, California 92083.

*JAZZERCISE T-Shirts: Short sleeve in mint green with dark green print, natural with dark brown print, navy with red print. Small, medium, large sizes. Long sleeve available in same colors and sizes. (Both are 50% polyester and 50% cotton.)

*JAZZERCISE props: hoops, wands, and ropes. Order from: Jazzercise, P.O. Box 1414, Vista, California 92083.

Send a stamped self-addressed envelope for price lists and ordering information.

Footwear and Bodywear worn by Judi in all pictures by Capezio Ballet Makers. Available at dance shops nationwide.

ABOUT THE AUTHORS

JUDI SHEPPARD MISSETT received her early dance training in Omaha, Nebraska, and Council Bluffs, Iowa. She holds a B.A. from Northwestern University School of Speech, where she also specialized in dance. She has danced professionally in musical comedies, summer stock, commercials, and industrial theater shows, and toured the United States and Europe with many dance and road companies—singing, dancing, and acting—as well as making television appearances. Judi's teaching credits include master classes for universities, colleges, and school districts in California and Illinois, as well as a host of classes in private studios, YMCAs, and city recreation programs. Judi is currently involved in training Jazzercise instructors in her special dance-fitness technique and setting up Jazzercise programs across the country.

DONA Z. MEILACH is a nationally known author-photographer. While living and working in Chicago, she coauthored the very successful *The Art of Belly Dancing*. When she moved to San Diego in 1975, she discovered Ms. Missett's classes and was immediately smitten by the approach to dance-exercise. Ms. Meilach is the author of over thirty how-to-do-it trend-setting arts and crafts books. She writes a syndicated column titled "Creative Crafts," and her articles on a variety of subjects appear in national magazines.